# THE REAL FORCE

## A 40-DAY DEVOTIONAL

PAUL KENT

WORTHY®
*Inspired*

Copyright © 2015 by Paul Kent

Published by Worthy Inspired, an imprint of Worthy Publishing Group, a division of Worthy Media, Inc., One Franklin Park, 6100 Tower Circle, Suite 210, Franklin, TN 37067.

WORTHY is a registered trademark of Worthy Media, Inc.

HELPING PEOPLE EXPERIENCE THE HEART OF GOD

eBook available wherever digital books are sold.

---

Library of Congress Control Number: 2015909925

---

Scripture references marked KJV are from the Holy Bible, King James Version

Scripture quotations are taken from the Holy Bible, New International Version®, NIV®. Copyright © 1973, 1978, 1984, 2011 by Biblica, Inc.™ Used by permission of Zondervan. All rights reserved worldwide. www.zondervan.com

This book has not been prepared, endorsed, or licensed by Lucasfilm LTD or any other person or entity affiliated with Lucasfilm, *Star Wars*, or related properties.

ISBN 978-1-61795-581-5

Cover Design by Chris Tobias / Tobias' Outerwear for Books
Page Layout by Bart Dawson

Printed in the United States of America

15 16 17 18 19 LBM 7 6 5 4 3 2 1

Praise for *The Real Force*

Paul Kent has written a great devotional book that combines the nostalgia of *Star Wars* with sound biblical truth.

Todd Aaron Smith,

Lucasfilm sketch card artist

If you've ever felt funny about enjoying the *Star Wars* movies so much, *The Real Force* offers some biblical parallels to redeem that guilty pleasure.

Luke Ridnour, NBA point guard

An inspiring devotional written by a true fan! Paul Kent quotes from the Scriptures and *Star Wars* canon with equal ease, and blends them together to bring out biblical truths embedded in the fascinating story of a galaxy far, far away.

Ed Strauss, author of

*A Hobbit Devotional*

Paul Kent does a remarkable (even ingenious) job marrying one of the most beloved movie series of all time with the most cherished Book of all time. Without taking the premise too far or forcing any predictable agenda, he weaves spiritual themes and biblical truths with elements of the time-honored films.

Trisha White Priebe, author of

*A Sherlock Holmes Devotional*

Reading this book will make you want to have a *Star Wars* movie marathon. This time though, you'll have a completely new biblical perspective.

Carlos Erazo, YouTuber—Proyecto GTG

*The Real Force* is the perfect devotional for a *Star-Wars*-literate generation embracing all things nerdy! Real-life lessons wrapped in a clever, saga-quoting package.

Jonathan McKee, author of *More Than Just the Talk* and<br>*The Guy's Guide to God, Girls and the Phone in Your Pocket*

To my wife, Laurie.
"I love you."
"I know."

# CONTENTS

# INTRODUCTION

DO YOU REMEMBER your first experience with *Star Wars*?

I sure do . . . and it was frustrating. You see, I wasn't allowed to watch it.

Depending on your age and church background, you might understand where I'm coming from. As an eleven-year-old kid in 1977, when Luke Skywalker and the crew took the world by storm, I wasn't supposed to patronize movie theaters. Mom and Dad held firm to our church's attitude against Hollywood films, and I was told "no" . . . over and over again.

That didn't stop me from buying *Star Wars* trading cards. Or the paperback novelization. Or an oversized comic book edition of the movie. I would even sit on our front porch at night, squinting at the Interstate 77 on-ramp lights across the river, imagining them as part of a *Star Wars* locale. I know, that's pretty sad.

But the Force must have been with me. Somehow, when *Star Wars* was re-released the following summer, Mom and Dad relented. They actually dropped me off at a theater to watch the movie. I had never experienced anything like the overhead passage of that massive Imperial Star Destroyer on the big screen. What a way to begin a movie series . . . and a lifelong enjoyment of the films.

Years later, as I dated the woman who would become my wife, I found that she, too, had enjoyed *Star Wars* . . . and before long we were popping in VCR tapes to watch the films together. Many times we've quoted movie phrases to each other: "Laugh it up, Fuzzball." "I find your lack of faith disturbing." "I recognized your foul stench." If either of us ever happens to say, "I'll be careful," the other quickly responds with the words of the ugly little man who threatened Luke in the Mos Eisley cantina, then found himself at the wrong end of Ben Kenobi's lightsaber: "You'll be dead!"

It struck me just recently, only a few weeks shy of my forty-ninth birthday, how much *Star Wars* remains a part of my imagination. Each day I exercise by riding my bicycle on a paved trail. At one point, I pedal through an eighty-yard tunnel under a highway. It has vertical walls and occasional round lights in the ceiling . . . and breezing through one morning I suddenly felt like Luke Skywalker skimming the trenches of the Death Star.

That's part of what makes *Star Wars* such fun. It's a memorable story of good and evil, featuring compelling leads, very cool special effects (especially for its day), and some occasional bad acting. How *did* they cast some of those minor characters, anyway?

Much has been written about the *Star Wars* series, by film critics, philosophers, even theologians, people trying to find deep meanings in every aspect of the series. Maybe those deep meanings are there . . . but I'm not watching the films for a Ph.D. dissertation. I just enjoy the experience.

Having said that, however, when I see particular movie scenes I'm often reminded of certain Bible verses. Not that the movies are "Christian" in their underlying perspective. But the larger themes—of duty, friendship, choices, good, and evil—are ideas that God Himself first explained in His Word. Many characters, events, and concepts in the *Star Wars* saga lend themselves to real-life spiritual parallels, thought-provoking takeaways that—if we really make them part of our lives—might actually improve us as human beings.

And that's why I've written *The Real Force: A 40-Day Devotional.* If you've read this far, I would guess you're a *Star Wars* fan. You're familiar enough with the films to know the basic story lines . . . or to quote many scenes verbatim. My hope is that the following readings will expose you to some previously unconsidered passages and realities from scripture. Or, if you already know the Bible truths, maybe this book will redeem the guilty pleasure of enjoying "just a movie" so much.

Really, that's the plan. Simple? Sure. Like the pleasure of watching that Imperial Star Destroyer glide across a movie screen.

PAUL KENT
Grand Rapids, Michigan

# A NOTE ON SOURCES

FOR DESCRIPTIONS and quotations in this book, I have drawn from three primary sources:

1. DVDs of the first six *Star Wars* films, including the 2008 Limited Editions of Episodes IV–VI
2. the official novelizations of the first six films, published by Ballantine Books/Del Rey
3. the movies' official website, StarWars.com

Though I will occasionally make reference to the "expanded universe" of *Star Wars* lore, this book is based on what some call the "canon" of the series, essentially the sources noted above. Generally, all descriptions and quotations are drawn from the films; if a book's details differ, this is noted in the text.

Throughout these entries, you'll find references to a fan survey I conducted between November 2014 and January 2015. Though not a scientific poll, the results indicate the likes and dislikes of more than one hundred everyday viewers, of both sexes, ranging in age from elementary school students to people in their fifties. Complete results of the survey can be found on a bonus website: realforcebook.com.

# DUST AND STARS

"Luminous beings are we . . .
not this crude matter."

**Yoda,** *The Empire Strikes Back*

AS PLANETS GO, Tatooine was nothing special. Its most famous native, Luke Skywalker, said as much to the newly-arrived C-3PO, whose first impression was of desolation. "If there's a bright center to the universe," Luke grumbled, "you're on the planet that it's farthest from." (Our fan survey participants were more upbeat, naming the planet their favorite Star Wars locale.)

Tatooine's landscape featured primarily sand and rock, with the occasional bleached-out skeleton to break up the monotony. In the heat of the planet's twin suns, people like Luke and his uncle, Owen Lars, were forced to wring whatever water they could from the atmosphere.

It wasn't just movie magic that created Tatooine, which appeared in all of the first six stories except *The Empire Strikes Back*: Filming took place in the northern African nation of Tunisia, whose southern reaches merge into the famed Sahara Desert. More recent political unrest in Tunisia led the producers of Episode VII to move filming of Tatooine scenes to the Middle Eastern emirate of Abu Dhabi.

In Episode IV, when C-3PO and his fellow droid R2-D2 landed on Tatooine as escapees from a star battle above, they were quickly rounded up by scavenging Jawas and sold to work on the Lars moisture farm. Artoo, however, carrying the stolen plans of the Empire's Death Star, had more important things to attend to—and promptly set off in search of Obi-Wan Kenobi.

Obi-Wan, a "crazy old man" in the opinion of Luke's uncle, had first landed on Tatooine as a much younger man, a Jedi-in-training under Qui-Gon Jinn. There, they found Anakin Skywalker, a young boy strong in the Force but slave to the disgusting junk dealer Watto.

Ruled by the likes of Jabba the Hutt, rife with gambling and violence, Tatooine was, as some say of their own less-than-sterling hometowns, "a good place to be from . . . *away* from." Anakin dreamed of escaping to the stars. Years later, Luke would share his unknown father's aspiration of leaving Tatooine, to shake "the dust off their feet," to borrow a biblical phrase (Acts 13:51).

Compared to the awe-inspiring stars, what is dust? As humans, we aspire to stardom—to be recognized for our brilliance or beauty or power. But we are literally dust: "The LORD God formed a man from the dust of the ground"

(Genesis 2:7). "For dust you are and to dust you will return" (Genesis 3:19).

Sometimes life itself seems grimy. It can be depressing to see all these people made of dust creating an atmosphere of figurative filth. Human beings lie, cheat, and steal. They selfishly take advantage of others. They pollute the world in every sense of the term. And too often, in our own moral and spiritual weakness, *we* contribute to that atmosphere ourselves.

An escape to the stars is very appealing. And very possible.

God "knows how we are formed, he remembers that we are dust," says Psalm 103:14. But the same psalm says He still loves us: "From everlasting to everlasting, the LORD's love is with those who fear him" (Psalm 103:17). Two verses further on, we see that "the LORD has established his throne in heaven" (Psalm 103:19). And through Jesus, God welcomes all of us to join Him there.

Tatooine was dusty and disreputable, a lot like we can be. But Tatooine was also a home to heroes, a place of relationships that changed lives . . . and an entire galaxy.

God sees that potential in each of us, too. As we obey Him and "work out" our salvation "with fear and trembling" (Philippians 2:12), we can become "blameless and pure, 'children of God without fault in a warped and crooked generation.'" And then we will "shine among them like stars in the sky" (Philippians 2:15).

> Those who are wise will shine like the brightness of the heavens, and those who lead many to righteousness, like the stars for ever and ever.
>
> Daniel 12:3

# TIGHT SPOTS

"Into the garbage chute, flyboy!"

**Princess Leia,** *Star Wars: A New Hope*

THE DEATH STAR trash compactor scene of Episode IV is a metaphor for life. Sometimes, in a world that's scary and dangerous enough by itself, you find that you're in a really tight spot. And, frankly, it stinks.

This sequence is one of many highlights of the original trilogy, featuring some of the series' most memorable lines. "Aren't you a little short for a stormtrooper?" Leia asks Luke as he bursts into cell 2187. Soon, trapped in the detention block hallway, she and Han Solo begin the insulting banter that will characterize their budding relationship:

"Looks like you managed to cut off our only escape route."

"Maybe you'd like it back in your cell, Your Highness."

"This is some rescue. You came in here, and you didn't have a plan for getting out?"

With the entire Death Star on alert and stormtroopers closing in, Leia takes charge of her own rescue. She grabs Luke's blaster to blow a hole where the wall and floor come together. The explosion jerks Han's attention away from the oncoming enemy, and he angrily demands to know what Leia is doing.

"Somebody has to save our skins," she yells back. "Into the garbage chute, flyboy!"

The princess jumps in first, followed by a reluctant Chewbacca. "Get in there, you big furry oaf," Han barks. "I don't care what you smell!" But once in the compactor himself, Han's attitude changes. "What an incredible smell you've discovered," he grumbles to Leia.

Of course, even the most casual fan knows what follows: The heroes find they can't blast their way out of the sealed chamber, and almost kill themselves with ricochets . . . they realize they're not alone in the pit, as a strange creature grabs Luke and pulls him under the filthy water . . . and, after Luke resurfaces, they hear an ominous sound that indicates the walls are beginning to move. Only the intervention of the droids, shutting down "all the garbage mashers on the detention level," saves the day.

Three Bible characters, Hananiah, Mishael, and Azariah, once found themselves in a similar situation. If you've ever been to Sunday school, you probably know them better as Shadrach, Meshach, and Abednego. As young Jewish nobles exiled in Babylon, they lived in a scary, dangerous world— a nation that had destroyed their homeland and now demanded they worship King Nebuchadnezzar's enormous golden idol.

They chose to rebel. For standing alone when all others bowed, they found themselves in a really tight spot—actually, a hot spot. On their way to the "fiery furnace," perhaps an ore smelter or brick kiln, they uttered some memorable lines: "If we are thrown into the blazing furnace, the God we serve is able to deliver us from it, and he will deliver us from Your Majesty's hand. But even if he does not, we want you to know, Your Majesty, that we will not serve your gods or worship the image of gold you have set up" (Daniel 3:17–18).

God saved the day for Shadrach, Meshach, and Abednego. But, as He often does, He delivered them *through,* not *from,* the flames. Jesus Himself had hoped to avoid the pain of the cross (Luke 22:39–42), but "for the joy set before him he endured" (Hebrews 12:2). James, thought by many to be Jesus' half brother, wrote that that's the way we should *all* view hardship: "Consider it pure joy, my brothers and sisters, whenever you face trials of many kinds, because you know that the testing of your faith produces perseverance. Let perseverance finish its work so that you may be mature and complete, not lacking anything" (James 1:2–4).

Tight spots aren't fun. Sometimes, they stink. But God has reasons for them, and He'll always be right there with us.

When you pass through the waters, I will be with you . . . . When you walk through the fire, you will not be burned.

Isaiah 43:2

# MASTER AND APPRENTICE

"Always two there are . . .
a master and an apprentice."

**Yoda,** *The Phantom Menace*

THE PRESIDENT has a vice president, the lead has an understudy, the starting pitcher has a reliever. And both Jedi and Sith masters have an apprentice.

It's all a kind of succession plan, except presidents, leads, starters, and Jedi don't typically kill their successors. With the Sith, you just never know.

On the dark side of the Force, apprenticeship is a double-edged sword—or lightsaber, as the case may be. The Sith master trains his pupil to draw raw power from hatred and aggression. But hatred, aggression, and raw power don't leave much room for loyalty, so this master-apprentice bond is tenuous at best.

Throughout the *Star Wars* saga, Darth Sidious is the master of evil. The alter ego of Chancellor Palpatine, he gained his position by killing his own master, Darth Plagueis. Although that is just a hint in Episode III, it's a plain statement in the *Revenge of the Sith* novelization. Sidious later ordered the execution of his apprentice Count Dooku. (With friends like *him,* who needs enemies?)

Another Sith apprentice, Darth Maul, provided movie-goers a glimpse into the dark side's power structure. The red-and-black-faced, horn-headed fiend, wielding a double-bladed lightsaber, conquered Jedi master Qui-Gon Jinn on the planet Naboo. But Darth Maul then fell victim to Qui-Gon's own apprentice, Obi-Wan Kenobi.

As the Jedi council mulled the mysterious warrior who had killed one of their greatest knights, Mace Windu told Yoda he believed it had been a Sith. With a knowing nod, Yoda replied, "Always two there are . . . a master and an apprentice."

The master and apprentice relationship occurs on the other side, as well—a notable example being Obi-Wan and his "Padawan learner" Anakin Skywalker. The elder commit-ted to training the younger, teaching the deepest truths of the Force and preparing the boy for success, it was hoped, as a Jedi knight.

In many ways, that illustrates the association between Jesus and His followers. Often called "Master" in Scripture (see Luke 5:5, 8:24, 9:49, 17:13; Colossians 4:1), Jesus has millions of "apprentices"—or, as they are known in the Bible, *disciples*—who learn the deep truths of God and pre-pare for success as His representatives in the world.

Since He is the infinite God, Jesus can provide perfectly individualized attention to His millions of followers. Always two there must be—each one of us and our Lord—because without Him, we are powerless to do good.

On the night of the "last supper," just before His betrayal and arrest, Jesus told His disciples, "I am the vine; you are the branches. If you remain in me and I in you, you will bear much fruit; apart from me you can do nothing" (John 15:5). What "fruit" will we grow when we "remain"? The fruit of the Holy Spirit, who Jesus would later send to live inside believers: "love, joy, peace, patience, kindness, goodness, faithfulness, gentleness, and self-control" (Galatians 5:22–23).

If we *don't* remain in Jesus—if we carelessly wander away or think we know better than Him or "just want to have some fun"—we risk a fall like Anakin Skywalker's, seduced by the dark side of life. In Galatians 5, the apostle Paul also noted the opposite of the fruit of the Spirit, which he called "the acts of the flesh." They're the destructive attitudes and behaviors so common to our world, things like sexual immorality, hatred, jealousy, selfish ambition, and drunkenness (see Galatians 5:19–21).

The "dark side of the Force" is fictional, but it illustrates an actual dark side of human nature—one that seeks to destroy us. With Jesus as our Master—as both the life-giving vine and "light of the world" (John 8:12)—that deathly darkness can be overcome. We must simply stay connected to Him.

> And now, dear children, continue in him, so that when he appears we may be confident and unashamed before him at his coming.
>
> 1 John 2:28

# AN ELEGANT WEAPON

"This weapon is your life."

**Obi-Wan Kenobi,** *Attack of the Clones*

BEFORE *STAR WARS,* plenty of movies had sword battles. But no one ever conceived duels quite like George Lucas did with the lightsaber.

As Obi-Wan Kenobi described it to Luke Skywalker, the lightsaber is "the weapon of a Jedi knight," used for a thousand generations to maintain peace and justice in the old Republic. Then came the dark era of the galactic Empire, due in large part to Luke's father.

When Luke meets Obi-Wan in the Jundland Wastes of Tatooine, he knows nothing of his father . . . nothing truthful, that is. Luke's uncle Owen had told the boy his father served as a navigator on a spice freighter. Obi-Wan adds to Luke's knowledge, but he's not entirely honest, either. As he hands over his old friend Anakin's lightsaber to Luke, Obi-Wan says, "Your father wanted you to have this."

In reality, Anakin Skywalker—having turned to the dark side and now calling himself Darth Vader—was unaware of his son . . . or of the boy's twin sister, Leia. Obi-Wan had taken Vader's lightsaber after defeating him in a dramatic duel amid the volcanoes of Mustafar. The old Jedi's deception, clearly designed to draw Luke into the rebellion, probably fell into the category of "true from a certain point of view." That was a phrase used to deflect Luke's anger after the boy learned Vader hadn't *killed* his father as Obi-Wan had said, but instead *was* his father.

The emotional conflict between father and son would explode into physical battles featuring lightsabers. Vader's crimson blade was characteristic of the evil Sith; Luke battled him on Cloud City with the blue-bladed Jedi sword Obi-Wan had carried away from Mustafar. Father bested son as he separated Luke from his lightsaber—and hand—both of which fell down a seemingly endless reactor shaft.

The next time they met, just before the battle of Endor, Luke had a prosthetic hand and a newly constructed, green-bladed lightsaber. This time, the son would separate the father from his lightsaber—and hand.

Besides their severed body parts, Luke and Vader left behind piles of wrecked handrails, computer terminals, and other equipment, to some extent contradicting Obi-Wan's claim that the lightsaber was less "clumsy or random" than a blaster. But perhaps the problem was more the era than the armament. In the time of a barbarous Empire, Obi-Wan described the lightsaber as "an elegant weapon for a more civilized age."

The Bible describes itself as a weapon, specifically the "sword of the Spirit" (Ephesians 6:17). It's certainly elegant, inscribed with those things God wants us to know about Himself, ourselves, sin, and salvation. This sword, though, was made for a completely *un*civilized age—that is, every era of human history.

In billions of lives since the fall of humanity, sin has separated people from their Creator and each other by corrupting us in our deepest selves. "The heart is deceitful above all things and beyond cure," the prophet Jeremiah wrote. "Who can understand it?" (17:9).

Jeremiah's answer is that God can. "I the LORD search the heart and examine the mind" (17:10) . . . and through His word, we can too: "The word of God is alive and active. Sharper than any double-edged sword, it penetrates even to dividing soul and spirit, joints and marrow; it judges the thoughts and attitudes of the heart" (Hebrews 4:12).

Scripture challenges all of us on something. Am I overly materialistic (Matthew 6:24; 1 Timothy 6:10)? Do I need to forgive an offense (Luke 17:3–4; Colossians 3:13)? How well do I care for the less fortunate (Matthew 25:31–40; James 1:27)? What is my ultimate goal in life (Matthew 22:34–40)? The Bible never lets us off easily, but it also promises great rewards—eternal rewards—for those of us who take God's Word seriously.

More than a quarter of the *Star Wars* fans who took our survey named the lightsaber as their favorite mechanical device in the films. Some even identified another parallel with God's Word: Not only is the lightsaber "totally cool," one said, "it is a source of light in darkness." See Psalm 119:105 for that connection.

If you recall, Luke Skywalker needed practice to enjoy the full benefit of his lightsaber. It's no different with the sword of the Spirit. Read the Bible regularly. Think about it through the day. Commit it to memory. If you need a place to start, try this:

I have hidden your word in my heart that I might not sin against you.

Psalm 119:11

# WILLING TO LISTEN

*"You must unlearn what you have learned."*

**Yoda,** *The Empire Strikes Back*

AS MUCH AS FOR their capability with a lightsaber, Jedi are known for their wisdom. But even Jedi and Jedi-to-be must learn to hear and accept the wise words of others.

Impatience and pride are common human traits, perhaps even more so in those with greater talent, intelligence, and capability. Consider the wrangling among Qui-Gon Jinn, Obi-Wan Kenobi, and the Jedi council over the status of young Anakin Skywalker.

Convinced he'd found "the chosen one," Qui-Gon brought the nine-year-old to the Jedi temple on Coruscant for an interview with Yoda and the rest of the order's leadership. When Mace Windu flatly stated the boy would *not* be trained as a Jedi, Qui-Gon was incredulous. "He is the chosen one. You must see it!"

Mace Windu voiced a concern that Yoda would echo years later with Luke Skywalker: "He is too old." For Yoda, the larger issue was Anakin's fear and anger. "Clouded this boy's future is," the old master murmured.

But Qui-Gon was not to be deterred. He suddenly announced that he would take Anakin as his Padawan learner, drawing a shocked glance from his apprentice Obi-Wan. Whatever hurt his unexpected replacement caused was quickly forgotten when Obi-Wan later saw Qui-Gon cut down by the Sith Lord Darth Maul.

"Promise me you will train the boy," the dying Qui-Gon begged, and Obi-Wan agreed. The promise would create more tension with Yoda, who was steadfast in his belief that Anakin's training was dangerous. When Obi-Wan told Yoda he would proceed "without the approval of the council, if I must," Yoda said he sensed Qui-Gon's "defiance" coming through. But Yoda reluctantly agreed to the council's decision to make Anakin Obi-Wan's apprentice.

Ultimately, Anakin's training made him extremely powerful—so when he turned to the dark side, he wreaked havoc on the Jedi order in particular and the galaxy in general. Every last Jedi should have listened to Yoda.

Nobody enjoys being told "no." We hate to hear the word as toddlers—and most of us still want our way in our twenties, thirties, forties . . . however long we live. But if we're honest, we'll all admit that at some time in our lives, we should have listened when someone tried to steer us clear of trouble and into better choices. "Those who disregard discipline despise themselves," the wise king Solomon wrote in Proverbs, "but the one who heeds correction gains understanding" (15:32).

Sometimes, we just need to admit that we don't know everything. Ever hear the story of Philip, the early evangelist, and an Ethiopian official who'd been visiting Jerusalem? The man was sitting in his chariot, reading aloud the prophecy of Isaiah. Philip hurried up to him and asked, "Do you understand what you are reading?" (Acts 8:30).

The Ethiopian didn't understand, though he could have pretended otherwise: "Oh, sure . . . I'm doing fine. Have a good day!" Instead, he asked for help: "How can I . . . unless someone explains it to me?" (Acts 8:31). He invited Philip into the chariot to talk; by the time Philip left, the Ethiopian believed in Jesus and had been baptized (Acts 8:32–40).

Jesus said our salvation requires humility: "Unless you change and become like little children, you will never enter the kingdom of heaven" (Matthew 18:3). That's also how growth occurs. God uses wise people to challenge and correct us . . . if we're humble enough to hear them, we become better.

Obi-Wan listened and learned. By Episode V, as a ghostly Force presence, he argued on Luke's behalf, telling Yoda that the boy would learn patience. When Yoda wanted to disqualify Luke for his anger, Obi-Wan asked, "Was I any different when you taught me?" When Yoda called Luke reckless, Obi-Wan recalled, "So was I, if you remember."

It's not unusual to struggle. But it's wise to listen and learn.

Whoever heeds life-giving correction will be at home among the wise.

Proverbs 15:31

# OBI-WAN'S SACRIFICE

"If you strike me down, I shall become more powerful than you can possibly imagine."

**Obi-Wan Kenobi,** *Star Wars: A New Hope*

IF YOU WATCH ONLY Episodes IV through VI, you might think of Obi-Wan Kenobi as a minor character. Important enough to propel Luke Skywalker on his heroic journey, and helpful in a bar fight, to be sure . . . but dying in the series' very first film, then appearing only in ghostly Force-moments in the next two.

Obi-Wan, however, is a dominant personality in Episodes I through III as friend and mentor of Anakin Skywalker, the "chosen one" around whom the entire storyline revolves. But Anakin's many weaknesses—his pride, fear, whining, and ultimate defection to the dark side—make him a far less sympathetic character than the noble, ever-courteous Obi-Wan, known for his warmth, wisdom, humor, and sacrifice.

Lest we equate his gentleness with weakness, remember that Obi-Wan Kenobi bested Darth Maul in a lightsaber clash; survived the huge, hideous acklay in the execution arena of Geonosis; defeated the alien bio-droid General Grievous in saber-to-saber, hand-to-hand, blaster-to-gut combat; and performed dozens of other courageous, selfless acts on behalf of individuals and the galaxy at large . . . all the while hating the space flight that his duty demanded.

That's the nature of sacrifice—serving a larger good, even when it's not easy or enjoyable.

Two other scenes epitomize Obi-Wan Kenobi's heart. Having overcome the attack—both physical and emotional—of his one-time friend Darth Vader on Mustafar, Obi-Wan oversaw the birth of Anakin's twins by the dying Padmé. Then, to keep Jedi hope alive, he offered to deliver the baby boy to Anakin's step-brother Owen Lars on Tatooine, and live nearby until the young Luke Skywalker was ready for training.

Nineteen years after that, with Luke, Han Solo, and Princess Leia trapped on the Empire's Death Star, Obi-Wan volunteered to disable the tractor beam that held the *Millennium Falcon* in thrall . . . and performed the ultimate sacrifice. On his way back to the *Falcon,* intercepted by Darth Vader, Obi-Wan dueled the dark lord just long enough to allow the rebels to reach the ship. Then, after telling Vader, "If you strike me down, I shall become more powerful than you can possibly imagine," he accepted his enemy's saber slash and simply disappeared, absorbed into the Force.

Like a soldier who falls on a primed grenade to save his mates, or a parent who leaps in front of a speeding car to shove a child to safety, Obi-Wan's selfless behavior is compelling and beautiful. "Old Ben" placed third in our fan survey of favorite characters (after Han Solo and Yoda, immediately ahead of Darth Vader, Luke Skywalker, and Boba Fett), with one respondent saying, "he's quietly powerful and sacrificial . . . I've always liked him, even when I was a child."

In the Bible, the apostle Paul described similar cases of self-sacrifice: "Very rarely will anyone die for a righteous person, though for a good person someone might possibly dare to die" (Romans 5:7). But, inspiring as they may be, these sacrifices are limited in their effect.

Paul went on to say, though, that "God demonstrates his own love for us in this: While we were still sinners, Christ died for us" (v. 8). Jesus' death on the cross was a sacrifice with eternal implications for every individual on earth. When Jesus "had offered for all time one sacrifice for sins, he sat down at the right hand of God," the book of Hebrews says. "For by one sacrifice he has made perfect forever those who are being made holy" (Hebrews 10:12, 14).

It was "the precious blood of Christ, a lamb without blemish or defect" (1 Peter 1:19) that met all the requirements of God's Old Testament laws about sacrifice for sin. And when we simply "believe in the Lord Jesus" (Acts 16:31), we are clean before God, adopted into His family, and able to live selfless lives in a terribly selfish world.

Jesus' ultimate sacrifice empowers us to make daily personal sacrifices—of the Obi-Wan variety—for others. Done for God, every one of them is compelling and beautiful.

> Then Jesus said to his disciples, "Whoever wants to be my disciple must deny themselves and take up their cross and follow me."
>
> Matthew 16:24

# IN TRAINING

"You are not a Jedi yet."

**Darth Vader,** *The Empire Strikes Back*

IS A COMPLIMENT followed by a "but" really a compliment?

Maybe that's the only kind of compliment to expect from the likes of Darth Vader.

In their first face-to-face meeting, the dark lord honored Luke Skywalker, saying, "The Force is with you." And then there's that *but*. "But you are not a Jedi yet."

Vader was right on both counts. As son of the "chosen one" Anakin Skywalker (though not yet aware of that fact), Luke *was* strong in the Force. And, having abandoned Yoda in hopes of rescuing Han Solo and Princess Leia, he was not truly a Jedi. "You must complete the training," the ancient master had implored Luke.

Yoda had good reason for concern. In the swamps of Dagobah, Luke had undergone strict Jedi preparation. He found more success, it seemed, with its physical than its mental aspects. Climbing vines, running through puddles, and flipping over tree roots, Luke improved his strength and agility, all the while toting Yoda on his back. Not one to waste an opportunity, the master leaned forward during the exercises to whisper Force truths into Luke's ear.

Much of Yoda's wisdom, unfortunately, missed its mark. When Luke's X-wing sank into the pond, he fussed over the impossibility of recovering it—and earned a masterful scolding. "Always with you it cannot be done," Yoda sighed. "Hear you nothing that I say?"

But dredging up a waterlogged starfighter was the least of Luke's worries. Yoda, with an assist from the ghostly spirit of Obi-Wan Kenobi, argued that Luke needed further training to evade the dark side of the Force. The evil way had seduced Darth Vader and the emperor, and they in turn would certainly use it on their inexperienced opponent. There would be no "quick and easy path," Yoda said, to Jedihood.

Nor is there a quick and easy path to Christian maturity. We who have believed in Jesus—the real Force—know that He is always with us (Hebrews 13:5). *But* . . . we are not yet all we can and should be. Getting there is a lifelong process the Bible calls sanctification, or growth in grace. Jesus Himself set the example, as a boy who "grew in wisdom and stature, and in favor with God and man" (Luke 2:52).

The apostle Paul wrote often of this growth, a process he experienced after a dramatic conversion on the road to Damascus. To that point a rabid hater of Jesus, the new Christian still known as Saul "grew more and more powerful and baffled the Jews living in Damascus by proving that Jesus is the Messiah" (Acts 9:22).

Later, to the church he'd founded in Corinth, Paul wrote, "Do you not know that in a race all the runners run, but only one gets the prize? Run in such a way as to get the prize. Everyone who competes in the games goes into strict training" (1 Corinthians 9:24–25). What kind of training? It goes beyond reading a devotional, although that is a start.

Growth in grace is powered by God, but demands our choice and effort. It begins with knowing what God wants, and that comes from reading—really studying—His word (2 Timothy 2:15). We pray to know God's will (Philippians 1:9–11). There's the denial of our own selfish desires (Matthew 16:24–25). We determine to "add to [our] faith goodness; and to goodness, knowledge; and to knowledge, self-control; and to self-control, perseverance; and to perseverance, godliness" (2 Peter 1:5–6).

Over time, we find ourselves becoming more like Jesus—not perfect yet, but stronger. And then one day, we'll hear His compliment without any qualification: "Well done, good and faithful servant!" (Matthew 25:21).

Grow in the grace and knowledge of our Lord and Savior Jesus Christ.

2 Peter 3:18

# GOOD OLD JAR JAR

"Mesa your humble servant."

**Jar Jar Binks,** *The Phantom Menace*

JAR JAR BINKS seemed to irritate Qui-Gon Jinn and movie-goers equally.

Banished from his underwater city of Otoh Gunga, Jar Jar was loitering on the surface of Naboo when the Trade Federation's droid army invaded. Clumsiness had gotten him kicked out of his home—and he promptly got into Qui-Gon's way as the Jedi master fled an oncoming transport.

"Get away! Get out of here!" Qui-Gon shouted at Jar Jar, who did neither. Jedi and Gungan collided, fell into a large puddle, and stayed low until the massive transport glided overhead. They could both be thankful the Trade Federation favored hovercraft technology.

Known for his "feel, don't think" approach to life, Qui-Gon lashed out at Jar Jar. "You almost got us killed!" he scolded. "Are you brainless?"

Offended, Jar Jar protested that he could speak—at which point Qui-Gon uttered an undeniable truth of life: "The ability to speak does not make you intelligent!"

Voiced by American actor Ahmed Best, the computer-generated Jar Jar Binks was identified by pop-culture website pastemagazine.com as "without a doubt, the worst CGI character of all time . . . utterly offensive in almost every respect."

Our fan survey found a similar aversion among everyday viewers, with the vast majority saying they either "found him annoying" or "hated him," and offering comments such as "ugh," "horrible character," and "low point of the saga."

At some point in life, we've all known a Jar Jar. Maybe it was that obnoxious kid who attached himself to you in junior high. Maybe it was the boss who only *thought* he was funny. Maybe it was a relative who always needed something from you. They're not terrible people . . . but they do drive you nuts.

Ever stop to think that God could probably view each of us that way?

Most of us aren't as bad as we could be. But we certainly all, as the apostle Paul put it, "fall short of the glory of God" (Romans 3:23). Even if we don't commit the "big" Ten-Commandment-style sins—idolatry, murder, adultery—all of us, at some time or another, will stumble on other things the Bible forbids. Maybe it's gossip, complaining, bitterness, love of money, unforgiveness, fear . . . there are any number of ways we can "grieve the Holy Spirit of God" (Ephesians 4:30).

And yet, God never views us the way young Obi-Wan Kenobi thought of Jar Jar: as "a pathetic life-form." To his credit, Obi-Wan said that with a slight smile. In His unending goodness and love, God "smiles" on us by showing grace when we fail.

Grace is an unearned kindness, and God's offer of salvation is the most dramatic example. When we accept that gift, we are "justified freely by his grace through the redemption that came by Christ Jesus" (Romans 3:24).

Then, going forward, God keeps showing His kindness as we inevitably fail. Because God himself, in the person of Jesus, lived on earth as a human being, He understands our struggles. "We do not have a high priest who is unable to empathize with our weaknesses, but we have one who has been tempted in every way, just as we are—yet he did not sin. Let us then approach God's throne of grace with confidence, so that we may receive mercy and find grace to help us in our time of need" (Hebrews 4:15–16).

And having gotten grace, we should give it. "Do not think of yourself more highly than you ought," Paul wrote to Christians in Rome. "Do not be proud, but be willing to associate with people of low position. Do not be conceited" (Romans 12:3, 16).

If you know a Jar Jar Binks, treat him kindly. You'll be imitating the God who shows you grace every day.

> Be completely humble and gentle; be patient, bearing with one another in love. Make every effort to keep the unity of the Spirit through the bond of peace.
>
> Ephesians 4:2–3

# THE WISDOM OF YODA

"Try not. Do. Or do not. There is no try."

**Yoda,** *The Empire Strikes Back*

IT'S UNCLEAR EXACTLY what kind of creature Yoda is. We know for sure that he's short, green, and very, very old. Pretty wise, too.

He's a revered master of the Jedi, part of the twelve-member council that meets on the capital planet of Coruscant. He's known both for the aforementioned wisdom and his adroitness with a lightsaber. He believes in peace but can lead troops in war. He's taught younger Jedi the ways of the Force for many, many years. Several centuries, in fact.

A key figure in the prequel films, Yoda does not appear in 1977's Episode IV. Debuting in *The Empire Strikes Back,* he's exiled on the swampy planet of Dagobah where Luke Skywalker journeys in search of Jedi training. Knowing only the name of Yoda, Luke doesn't recognize the quirky little creature who meets him—and is quickly annoyed by Yoda's antics.

It's not until the exasperated master mutters, "I cannot teach him . . . the boy has no patience!" that Luke realizes just who he's found. Hoping to salvage his bungled interview, Luke insists, "I am ready . . . I can be a Jedi." Yoda's response? "What know you ready? For eight hundred years have I trained Jedi. My own counsel will I keep on who is to be trained."

With the disembodied voice of Obi-Wan arguing on Luke's behalf, Yoda finally concedes and agrees to train his impatient visitor. They will have a rocky relationship as master and apprentice, with Luke's quick temper and irritability often confirming Yoda's reluctance to invest time and energy in this son of Anakin Skywalker. Yoda knows at this point what the young man does not: Luke is the biological son of "the chosen one," the miraculously-conceived human being who was supposed to bring balance to the Force but instead landed squarely on its dark side.

Like his father, now known as Darth Vader, Luke is naturally powerful in the Force. But like the younger version of his father, the pre-fall Anakin, Luke is also easily frustrated, quick to place blame, even defeatist at times. These negative traits lead to one of the series' great teachable moments—and the number one result in our fan survey of favorite Star Wars lines.

When Luke's starfighter becomes a submarine, sinking to the bottom of a Dagobah swamp, he grumbles, "We'll never get it out now."

Sighing, Yoda reminds Luke of the Jedi training that

included moving rocks with his mind. "Moving stones around is one thing," Luke retorts. "This is totally different."

Pounding his gimer stick on the ground, Yoda insists there is no difference—the problem is entirely in Luke's attitude. Chastened, Luke reluctantly agrees to "give it a try."

"No!" Yoda responds. "Try not. Do. Or do not. There is no try."

You'll find Yoda's wisdom on posters and coffee mugs, T-shirts and yoga pants (seriously). And you'll find his words all over the Internet. Why? Because they challenge the self-defeating attitude many of us wrestle with. "I'll try" implies half-heartedness, an assumption that our efforts will not succeed.

If you're going to pursue anything of value—a relationship, an education, a career, whatever type of achievement—you should, as the apostle Paul says, "work at it with all your heart, as working for the Lord, not for human masters" (Colossians 3:23).

Our spiritual aspirations fall into this category, too. Jesus Himself criticized His followers in the city of Laodicea, now ruins in western Turkey, for being "lukewarm." They were in the "give it a try" mode, but Jesus said "you are neither cold nor hot. I wish you were either one or the other!" (Revelation 3:15). In other words, "Do. Or do not."

Of course, Jesus wasn't saying the Laodiceans should be cold spiritually, that a choice of "do not" for faith was acceptable. But in contrasting that option with the hot, "do" kind of faith, He was saying a lukewarm, "I'll try" Christianity is just as chilly and dead. And He added, somewhat ominously, "I am about to spit you out of my mouth" (Revelation 3:16).

That's the bad news. The good news is that Jesus offers a way up and out. It starts with our own mind-set (the "do") and ends, as always, with His power and provision. "Be earnest and repent," He says. "Here I am! I stand at the door and knock. If anyone hears my voice and opens the door, I will come in and eat with that person, and they with me" (Revelation 3:19–20).

Don't just try to live the Christian life. Make a commitment to do what's right—and God himself will give the success.

> He who began a good work in you will carry it on to completion until the day of Christ Jesus.
>
> Philippians 1:6

# JUST A CLONE

> "Who's the more foolish,
> the fool or the fool who follows him?"
>
> **Obi-Wan Kenobi,** *Star Wars: A New Hope*

EARLY IN *STAR WARS,* released in 1977, both Luke Skywalker and Princess Leia (as a holographic image) mention the Clone Wars. It would be twenty-five years before moviegoers really knew what they were talking about.

The mysterious references occur in the desert home of "Ben" Kenobi, after Luke and C-3PO track R2-D2 through the dangerous Jundland Wastes. Artoo was determined to deliver Leia's message to the man Luke's Uncle Owen called a "wizard." But in Obi-Wan Luke finds not only a Jedi knight but information on his own family history. Viewers, meanwhile, are left to ponder those clones.

The puzzle's answer unfolds slowly in the 2002 prequel *Attack of the Clones*. Investigating an assassination attempt on Senator Amidala, a decades-younger Obi-Wan—with Scottish actor Ewan MacGregor in the role made famous by London-born Alec Guinness—tracks a clue to the distant water-world of Kamino. There, he finds the willowy, white-skinned Kaminoans preparing an army of clones 1.2 million strong, supposedly for the Republic's use at the request of a Jedi master.

Actually, the clone army is part of an elaborate plot by Chancellor Palpatine—the public face of the evil Darth Sidious—to assume dictatorial power over a new galactic empire. Ultimately, he will use the clones to destroy the greatest obstacle to his ambitions: the Jedi order.

The clones are the genetic offspring of the tough, clever bounty hunter, Jango Fett. Birthed in the sterile hatcheries of the Kaminoans ("them cloners," in the words of Obi-Wan's friend and informant Dexter Jettster), individual soldiers are modified to age at twice the normal human rate . . . and be more docile than their progenitor. They would be resourceful fighters like Jango but more willing to take orders.

In their training and dining rooms, Obi-Wan sees groups of clones produced five and ten years earlier, with individuals who appear to be ten and twenty years of age. As he struggles to make sense of it all, you can almost sense Obi-Wan's disgust for a process that creates countless beings almost exactly the same . . . and just a little bit less than human.

Sadly, that's a good description for what the Bible calls the "natural man" (1 Corinthians 2:14 KJV), human beings before they truly understand and accept Jesus Christ as Lord. Natural men (or women) often proudly believe they're being their "own person" but are really conformed "to the pattern of this world" (Romans 12:2).

What is that pattern? The dreary sameness we see in the political realm, the entertainment world, the business arena, the educational system, occasionally even in ourselves . . . behaviors the prophet Isaiah wrote about upwards of three thousand years ago: People known for their parties and music and wine but who "have no regard for the deeds of the LORD, no respect for the work of his hands . . . who call evil good and good evil . . . who are wise in their own eyes and clever in their own sight . . . who acquit the guilty for a bribe, but deny justice to the innocent" (Isaiah 5:12, 20–21, 23). Even those who don't know God realize we're a little less than human when we act this way.

That's why the apostle Paul urged believers to "be transformed by the renewing of your mind" . . . to "hate what is evil; cling to what is good" . . . to "honor one another above yourselves" (Romans 12:2, 9–10). As we do these things, we rise above our human clone status, finding our true identity and destiny in our amazing, infinite God. When we believe in Jesus, the image of God in us—so messed up by sin—is able to shine again. And our true individuality is allowed to blossom.

Never settle for being "just a clone."

We all, who with unveiled faces contemplate the Lord's glory, are being transformed into his image with ever-increasing glory, which comes from the Lord, who is the Spirit.

2 Corinthians 3:18

# BETTER SAFE THAN . . .

> "Evacuate? In our moment of triumph?"
>
> **Grand Moff Tarkin,** *Star Wars: A New Hope*

TO THE ROLE OF the Grand Moff Tarkin, Peter Cushing brought cheek bones sharp enough to cut paper—and an understated menace as he rolled the R's in "crush the rebellion."

The venerable actor had portrayed characters from Sherlock Holmes to Dr. Who in British films of the 1950s, '60s, and '70s. He was well known for horror movies before landing his most famous role as commander of the Death Star in Episode IV in 1977. Cushing died in 1994 at age eighty-one.

Grand Moff Tarkin, however, perished in the Death Star's demise. And he could never say that he hadn't been warned.

Darth Vader had declared the station's vulnerability during a memorable argument with Admiral Motti. The mighty weapon wasn't the "ultimate power in the universe," as Motti claimed. Vader said the Force was superior and provided a taste of that truth by cutting off Motti's argument—and air flow—by raising his black-gloved hand in a choking gesture. Gasping, Motti clawed helplessly at his collar until Tarkin intervened.

When Vader discerned the presence of his old Jedi teacher, Obi-Wan Kenobi, the hunters began to feel hunted. Later in the movie, this sensation became reality as X- and Y-wing fighters of the rebellion swooped down for an attack.

In the Death Star's control room, an Imperial officer advised Tarkin that an analysis had shown the tiny ships did indeed pose a danger to the giant station. "Should I have your ship standing by?" he asked.

"Evacuate? In our moment of triumph?" Tarkin responded. "I think you overestimate their chances!"

Was the Grand Moff's incredulous look and tone a show of bravado? Or was he truly oblivious to the danger? Whatever the case, the results were bad. Tarkin would have done well to heed the warnings.

That's true in all our lives. When warning flags are raised, we do well to consider them.

Human nature is such that advice, even when we ask for it, is tough to accept. Think about it: Have you ever chosen to pursue your own plans no matter what your friends or family—or the Bible—had to say? If you've never done that yourself, have you watched someone else? How did it work out?

In the Bible, Rehoboam became king of Israel when his father, Solomon, died. Early on, the people of Israel asked

Rehoboam to ease the "heavy yoke" of taxes and labor his father had imposed, and the older, wiser government officials urged the new king to agree. "If today you will be a servant to these people and serve them and give them a favorable answer, they will always be your servants" (1 Kings 12:7).

That was good advice . . . but Rehoboam listened instead to his foolish young friends, who counseled steel. "My father made your yoke heavy; I will make it even heavier," he told the people. "My father scourged you with whips; I will scourge you with scorpions" (1 Kings 12:14).

Not wise. Rehoboam's choice split the kingdom and led to "continual warfare" (1 Kings 14:30) with his counterpart Jeroboam. Their nations, Judah and Israel, respectively, would suffer spiritually, morally, and politically for generations before being overrun by other world powers.

In the book of Proverbs, wisdom is personified as a woman. She laments that people "disregard all my advice and do not accept my rebuke" (Proverbs 1:25). As with the Grand Moff Tarkin, there's a bad result in Scripture as well: "I in turn will laugh when disaster strikes you" (Proverbs 1:26).

If that seems negative, it is. But Proverbs 1 ends positively: "Whoever listens to me will live in safety and be at ease, without fear of harm" (Proverbs 1:33).

How do we get that wisdom that keeps us from trouble? It begins with listening to God—and He speaks through the Bible. Whether you're just a kid or you're older than Yoda, you'll find life-giving, life-enhancing, life-*preserving* wisdom in the pages of that incredible book.

> The fear of the LORD is the beginning of wisdom; all who follow his precepts have good understanding.
>
> Psalm 111:10

# DROID ROLES

> "Vaporators? Sir, my first job was programming
> binary load lifters, very similar to
> your vaporators in most respects."
>
> **C-3PO,** *Star Wars: A New Hope*

IN THE *STAR WARS* universe, you can't swing a womp-rat without hitting a droid.

Often called "robots" in other films, these mechanical marvels were built to serve humans and other life forms in dangerous, difficult, or simply day-to-day jobs. "Protocol droids" like C-3PO work to smooth relations among the galaxy's many species, using their programming in etiquette and language. Always a talker, Threepio spoke the very first lines in the *Star Wars* saga: "Did you hear that?" he asks fellow droid R2-D2 in a rebel cruiser under Empire attack. "They shut down the main reactor. We'll be destroyed for sure."

Unable to speak, but capable of most anything else, Artoo comes from the "astromech" class. He popped up throughout our fan survey, earning spots on several lists: "favorite character," "favorite non-human character," and "favorite mechanical device."

Short and barrel-shaped, astromechs use a variety of tool-tipped appendages to manage and fix spacecraft . . . though R2-D2 also has a knack for saving his human friends' skin. In a long and eventful career, he won honor for repairing Queen Amidala's damaged transport, defending Anakin Skywalker's fighter from an enemy "buzz droid," carrying the stolen Death Star plans, helping Luke Skywalker destroy said Death Star, even smuggling Luke's lightsaber into Jabba the Hutt's palace for the rescue of Han Solo and Princess Leia. And did we mention that Artoo can read most anybody's computer system, swim through swamps, even fly when needed? No wonder he claimed the Number 1 spot on TotalFilm.com's list of the "50 Greatest Movie Robots."

Scan the galaxy, and you'll see plenty of others doing their thing, those specific tasks they were designed for:

- pit droids servicing pod racers on Tatooine;
- the SP-4 analysis droid, helping Obi-Wan Kenobi in the Jedi Temple;
- skinny, not-overly-bright battle droids and their fearsome, heavy-infantry cousins, the droidekas, doing the Separatist Alliance and Trade Federation's dirty work;
- probe droids, searching Mos Espa for Padmé and Hoth for the Rebel base, dispatched by Darths Maul and Vader, respectively;

- surgeon droids like Too-Onebee (2-1B), assisting Luke Skywalker at both the beginning and end of *The Empire Strikes Back*;
- even a waitress droid, wiping down tables at Dex's Diner in lower Coruscant.

With his humanoid arms, C-3PO might have wiped down tables at Dex's—though that would have been a poor use of his other, more advanced skills. Interestingly, that's very similar to a situation Jesus' twelve apostles once found themselves in.

In the early days of the church—shortly after Jesus had returned to heaven and sent the Holy Spirit to believers on earth—the apostles decided they needed help to distribute food to widows. "It would not be right for us to neglect the ministry of the word of God in order to wait on tables," they said (Acts 6:2).

Were they saying they were too important for "menial tasks"? Not at all. They were recognizing the varying skill sets—what the Bible calls "gifts"—that God gives His followers. "Just as each of us has one body with many members, and these members do not all have the same function" the apostle Paul told the church in Rome, "so in Christ we, though many, form one body, and each member belongs to all the others. We have different gifts, according to the grace given to each of us" (Romans 12:4–6).

Like the apostles, some Christians today are called to preach and teach. Others are meant to serve, encourage, give, lead, or show mercy (vv. 6–8). If you love to speak God's Word publicly, great. But if you'd rather duel a droideka than sing a solo, that's okay, too. Up-front or behind the scenes, find a way to serve that suits who God made you to be.

It's what you were built for.

> There are different kinds of gifts, but the same Spirit distributes them. There are different kinds of service, but the same Lord. There are different kinds of working, but in all of them and in everyone it is the same God at work.
>
> 1 Corinthians 12:4–6

# IN THE BACKGROUND

"Red Ten, standing by."

*Star Wars: A New Hope*

LUKE, HAN, LEIA . . . Obi-Wan, Vader, Yoda . . . Amidala, Windu, Palpatine . . .

You immediately recognize many Star Wars characters by name or face. But there are scores of lesser characters who fill out the storyline and complete the movies.

So here's a quick quiz: Are you fan enough to identify the film and actor for background figures like Major Derlin and Sabé?

Derlin appears in *The Empire Strikes Back* as a Rebel officer on Hoth. While Princess Leia describes the evacuation mission to a group of orange-suited pilots, he stands by quietly in a tan uniform, large goggles perched on the bill of his hat. When Leia finishes, Derlin—in real life, actor John Ratzenberger—claps his hands and shouts, "Everybody to your stations. Let's go!"

In the years following, Ratzenberger would gain fame for his role as mail carrier Cliff Claven in the 1980s sitcom *Cheers*. And after that, he would voice a character in every computer-animated Pixar film, from *Toy Story*'s Hamm the piggy bank to the Abominable Snowman in the two "Monsters" films.

The name *Sabé* offers a clue as to her film. In *The Phantom Menace,* the queen of Naboo—Padmé Amidala—had a group of five handmaidens, each with the same treatment on the final *e*: Rabé, Eirtaé, Yané, Saché, and Sabé. The actress portraying Sabé went on to stardom opposite Johnny Depp in the *Pirates of the Caribbean* movies: Keira Knightley. (Though in *The Phantom Menace* credits, her name is spelled "Kiera.")

As with any movie, many if not most roles are filled by relatively unknown actors, the kind who might jog an occasional thought of "where did I see her before?" Or maybe not. The character of Zam Wesell, who tries to kill Padmé in Episode II, is played by an Australian actress, Leeanna Walsman. Luke Skywalker's Aunt Beru, like Obi-Wan Kenobi, appears in both older and younger versions in the first two trilogies. She is portrayed by English actress Shelagh Fraser in 1977, by Australian Bonnie Maree Piesse in 2002 and 2005.

And then there are those actors so disguised by costumes or makeup that you'd never recognize them from film to film. That was certainly true of English little person Jack Purvis, who portrayed the chief Jawa in Episode IV, an

Ugnaught in *The Empire Strikes Back,* and an Ewok in *Return of the Jedi.*

For every Luke Skywalker, there are many Major Derlins, Sabés, Aunt Berus, and Jawas. Without the background folks, the stars don't shine as brightly.

It's a lot like that in the Christian world, too . . . though all the shining should be done for God, not ourselves. The vast majority of Christians are not "stars" like Billy Graham or whatever other leader you most admire. And it's always been that way.

On the day of Pentecost, when God sent the Holy Spirit to live in Jesus' followers, Peter preached to a huge crowd in Jerusalem. The book of Acts says, "Those who accepted his message were baptized, and about three thousand were added to their number that day" (Acts 2:41).

Peter was the star whose story we remember; his supporting cast of three thousand is almost completely unknown. But consider that those backgrounders form the core of the Christian faith we share in today. Behind the scenes, they told family, friends, and neighbors about Jesus . . . and God's great story spread around the world.

If you're one of God's superstars, great. But if you're in the background, that's perfectly okay, too. You're in good company. Every one of us is important to the production.

Brothers and sisters, think of what you were when you were called. Not many of you were wise by human standards; not many were influential; not many were of noble birth. But God chose the foolish things of the world to shame the wise; God chose the weak things of the world to shame the strong.

1 Corinthians 1:26–27

# ET TU, DOOKU?

"Twice the pride, double the fall."

**Count Dooku,** *Revenge of the Sith*

ONCE A JEDI KNIGHT, Count Dooku walked away in apparent disgust . . . not so much with the Jedi themselves as with the galactic republic they served as peacekeepers.

"Political idealist" is how Ki-Adi-Mundi, the Jedi knight with the soaring forehead, described Dooku. The count would lead thousands of star systems to withdraw from the Republic over corruption in the senate. The Separatist movement caused confusion and concern among the Jedi and loyal senators such as Padmé Amidala.

When she was targeted for assassination, Padmé speculated that Count Dooku was behind the attempt. Ki-Adi-Mundi and Mace Windu both disagreed, feeling that Dooku's character and Jedi training argued against the possibility. Their optimistic appraisal was sadly mistaken.

A handsome face, a smooth bass voice, and a suave style aided Dooku's political maneuvering. They also obscured a scheming heart that had gone all the way over to the dark side.

Though he had been trained by the great Yoda, the count ultimately sided with the evil Darth Sidious, taking the name Darth Tyranus and helping to engineer the Clone Wars. Sidious and Tyranus were playing three sides against each other—the Republic, the Separatists, and the Trade Federation—and all of them against the Jedi order. When the ashes of the conflagration had cooled, Sidious planned to be dictator of a new galactic empire.

Count Dooku would never enjoy that day, finding to his horror that evil apprentices are expendable. When Sidious—in reality, the Republic's Chancellor Palpatine—learned of a coming "chosen one," he schemed to turn Anakin Skywalker to the dark side . . . and goaded him to kill Dooku. A key player in Episodes II and III, the count gained not a single mention in our fan survey of favorite *Star Wars* characters.

Perhaps Dooku's original motives were pure. But at some point, he crossed the line to an outright betrayal of all that was right and good. And his former supporters could ask the question that Shakespeare's Julius Caesar directed to his friend Brutus, coming in a crowd to assassinate the Roman emperor: "*Et tu*?" "And you?"

Jesus asked a similar question to one of His twelve disciples, who sold out the Lord with a sign of friendship: "Judas, are you betraying the Son of Man with a kiss?"

(Luke 22:48). Though God used an ugly human choice to accomplish a beautiful divine salvation, Judas Iscariot's betrayal caused a lot of pain and grief . . . as does the failure of believers today. That's why it's so important to "hold unswervingly to the hope we profess" (Hebrews 10:23). No matter how small and, we may think, insignificant our choices are, they can lead to larger failures of devastating impact.

Every day, we make ethical and moral decisions—whether to be honest in our business dealings, whether to keep our relationships pure, whether to base our lives on something higher than society's standards. The real question is this: Will we live our lives according to God's commands, as He's shown us in the Bible?

We should be leery of any choice that pulls us from the plain truth of Scripture. Think of King Solomon, who was "wiser than anyone else" (1 Kings 4:31), but who indulged his lust for women, with terrible results. "They were from nations about which the Lord had told the Israelites, 'You must not intermarry with them, because they will surely turn your hearts after their gods.' Nevertheless, Solomon held fast to them in love. He had seven hundred wives of royal birth and three hundred concubines, and his wives led him astray" (1 Kings 11:2–3). As we should always expect, God's prediction proved true: Solomon eventually worshipped idols (1 Kings 11:4–5).

If, as many believe, Solomon wrote the book of Ecclesiastes, it appears that he ultimately returned to the Lord. Redemption, unfortunately, was impossible for Count Dooku. Better for us that we never turn away at all.

> . . . holding on to faith and a good conscience, which some have rejected and so have suffered shipwreck with regard to the faith.
>
> 1 Timothy 1:19

# NO EXCUSES

"I am a Jedi, like my father before me."

**Luke Skywalker,** *Return of the Jedi*

LUKE SKYWALKER LONGED to leave Tatooine. So when Ben Kenobi urged him to join the galactic rebellion, Luke jumped at the chance.

Well, not really. Luke actually made excuses for staying put.

Growing up in a harsh, sprawling desert, Luke dreamed of trading the vaporators and condensers of Uncle Owen's moisture farm for the excitement of "the Academy." That's the *Imperial* Academy, mind you, where Luke's friend Biggs Darklighter became a star pilot before defecting to the rebels' side. Though he flew in the Death Star attack sequence, his backstory was not included in the original movie release. Biggs' desire to "jump ship and join the Alliance" is explained in the *Star Wars* novelization.

Moviegoers were left to discern Luke's motivations from comments made early in Episode IV. When his uncle forbade a trip to see friends in Tosche Station, Luke grumbled, "Biggs is right . . . I'm never gonna get out of here." When

C-3PO mentioned his own experience with the Alliance, Luke excitedly asked for information. After cleaning up Threepio and R2-D2, Luke told Owen that if the droids were successful on the farm, he wanted to apply to the Academy within the year. Shortly after that, Luke told Ben Kenobi that he hated the Empire.

But that last comment was halfhearted, an attempt to evade Obi-Wan's sudden, shocking challenge: "You must learn the ways of the Force if you're to come with me to Alderaan." Getting off Tatooine was exactly the goal Luke claimed. But when opportunity knocked, fear bolted the door.

"I can't get involved," Luke told Ben. There was work to do. The Empire and the rebellion against it were really far away. This just wasn't the time. "It's not that I like the Empire," Luke assured Obi-Wan. It was just that . . . there were reasons to stick around home.

Excuses ruled—until Imperial storm troopers, tracking C-3PO and R2-D2, slaughtered Luke's aunt and uncle. At that point, all reasons for delay and resistance disappeared. "There's nothing for me here now," Luke said, agreeing to accompany Ben to Alderaan. He would become a Jedi and oppose the evil Empire.

One of the Bible's great leaders approached his calling in a similar way. When God picked Moses to lead Israel out of its slavery in Egyptian, he argued—several times. "Who am I that I should go to Pharaoh?" "What if they do not believe me?" "I have never been eloquent." "Please send someone else" (Exodus 3:11; 4:1, 10, 13).

Moses' reluctance almost got him killed (see Exodus 4:24). But finally, with his brother Aaron as a spokesman, Moses obeyed. And he changed the course of history.

Though few of us will have that level of impact, God wants all of us to do something. He often calls, though we do have the freedom to make excuses. We are not clone troopers, engineered to obey without question.

But if God rarely compels, He is happy to *convince* us to serve—and He has the most amazing resources to bring to bear. Think of Jonah, who resisted God's call but came to his senses "inside the fish" (Jonah 2:1).

Popular books and speakers—Christian and otherwise—encourage us to view life as a continual adventure. It might be for a handful like Luke Skywalker, Moses, or Jonah. But for most, the Bible's call to "live peaceful and quiet lives" (1 Timothy 2:2) is more realistic. If God wants you to run for president, climb the tallest mountains, or lead the next Great Awakening, wonderful—by all means, do that. But for the great majority of us, the calling is likely more modest . . . to change a job, get involved at church, exercise, adopt a child, help out a neighbor, break a bad habit.

Whatever the call, if God says "go," just go. No excuses.

The LORD said to [Moses], "Who gave human beings their mouths? Who makes them deaf or mute? Who gives them sight or makes them blind? Is it not I, the LORD? Now go; I will help you speak and will teach you what to say."

Exodus 4:11–12

# EWOKS . . . SERIOUSLY?

"Short help's better than no help at all."

**Han Solo,** *Return of the Jedi*

SOMEHOW, AFTER ALL the soaring space drama of Episodes IV and V, the forest-based Ewoks of Episode VI just didn't seem to fit. That was especially true when what appeared to be a plush-toy marketing tie-in defeated the armored troopers of the mighty galactic empire.

In fairness, it should be said that some of our fan survey respondents did name Ewoks as their favorite non-human creatures in the *Star Wars* series—about as many as identified Jawas or Jabba the Hutt. These "sentient furred bipeds," in the description of the official Star Wars website, were certainly valiant, aiding the rebellion in the battle of Endor that destroyed the unfinished but "fully armed and operational" Death Star II.

The Ewoks lived in primitive huts built high into the tall trees of their moon, the actual name of which is debated by true *Star Wars* geeks. When the rebels' Admiral Ackbar mentioned "the forest moon of Endor," did he mean "the forest moon (named) Endor" or "the (unnamed) forest moon of (the planet) Endor"? Whatever the place was called, when

Luke Skywalker and Han Solo visited, they found the Ewoks were not to be trifled with. Captured at spear point, bound hand and foot, and carried on poles between the furry creatures, the men would have become dinner but for the intervention of C-3PO, who the Ewoks viewed as a god. Many found it all silly.

In a 2008 article for the movie magazine *Premiere*, interviewer Brantley Bardin called the Ewoks "loathsome," and interviewee Harrison Ford agreed. "I hated 'em, too—it was like a teddy bear prom."

Nearly every movie requires the "willing suspension of disbelief," a phrase the English poet Samuel Taylor Coleridge coined in the early 1800s. The *Star Wars* films are no exception . . . though some elements of the series demand more suspending than others. The Ewoks' action movie equivalent might be an unarmed, off-duty cop who takes down a whole platoon of German terrorists . . . who, luckily, can't hit the broad side of a semi-truck with a machine gun.

In real life, we find that God often uses the ridiculous to accomplish His plans. The Bible actually calls some of God's own key storylines "foolish"—from the human point of view. Here's how the apostle Paul describes them:

- "The message of the cross is foolishness to those who are perishing, but to us who are being saved it is the power of God" (1 Corinthians 1:18).

- "Since in the wisdom of God the world through its wisdom did not know him, God was pleased through the foolishness of what was preached to save those who believe" (1 Corinthians 1:21).

- "We preach Christ crucified: a stumbling block to Jews and foolishness to Gentiles" (1 Corinthians 1:23).

- "The person without the Spirit does not accept the things that come from the Spirit of God but considers them foolishness, and cannot understand them because they are discerned only through the Spirit" (1 Corinthians 2:14).

God uses not only His "foolish" ideas but weak and insignificant people to do great things in the world. In the time of ancient Israel's judges, God called a man named Gideon to save His people from the enemy Midianites. Gideon's response? "How can I save Israel? My clan is the weakest in Manasseh, and I am the least in my family." God's answer? "I will be with you" (Judges 6:15–16).

When God is with you, He gives you the wisdom and strength you need to do whatever it is that He wants. It doesn't matter if you're a Gideon, an Ewok . . . or an everyday *Star Wars* fan.

For the foolishness of God is wiser than human wisdom, and the weakness of God is stronger than human strength.

1 Corinthians 1:25

# A WORLD OF TROUBLE

"You will never find a more wretched hive of scum
and villainy. We must be cautious."

**Obi-Wan Kenobi,** *Star Wars: A New Hope*

WOULD YOU LAUGH as someone threatened to blow you
to pieces? Would you compliment your potential killer on
his boldness and creativity? If you were Jabba the Hutt,
you would.

In Jabba's palace on Tatooine, a small but confident
bounty hunter barges into a noisy party. Boushh approaches
the powerful gangster, leading a shackled Chewbacca—
the best friend and business partner of Jabba's "favorite
decoration," the carbon-encased Han Solo. Boushh demands
fifty thousand, twice the Hutt's offer, for the mighty
Wookiee. "Why?" Jabba asks. "Because he's holding a thermal detonator!" C-3PO reports, each perfectly-enunciated
word tinged with robotic fear.

Jabba the Hutt is ugly, unscrupulous, and utterly disgusting, but you would never say that to his very large
face. A crime boss known throughout the galaxy but head-
quartered on Luke Skywalker's home planet, it was Jabba
who unwittingly pushed Han Solo into the rebellion against

the Empire. When he met Luke and Obi-Wan seeking passage to Alderaan, Han was scrambling for cash to pay off a debt to Jabba.

Named but not shown in the 1977 release of *Star Wars*, Jabba does appear in the twentieth-anniversary special edition rechristened as Episode IV, *A New Hope*. A sequence featuring Han and Jabba, cut from the original film, was reinserted with a new, computer-generated Hutt. Some purists disparage the scene, preferring the physical puppet used in 1983's Episode VI, *Return of the Jedi*. Which brings us back to situation described above . . . .

Faced with certain death, Jabba's retinue reacts in terror, covering their faces or diving behind furniture. The fearsome bounty hunter Boba Fett whips out his weapon. Jabba himself just chuckles.

"This bounty hunter is my kind of scum," the gangster rumbles in Huttese, "fearless and inventive." Jabba counteroffers with 35,000, Boushh agrees, and the party picks up where it left off.

Ultimately, it appears that Jabba knew Boushh was Princess Leia in disguise, attempting to rescue Han. Jabba shows up—laughing again—as Leia unfreezes her love. Both end up in the Hutt's custody, as will Luke Skywalker, arriving shortly on his own rescue mission.

For Christians, life in this world can feel something like that—with the good guys under the gun while the Jabbas, the Bobas, and the other troublemakers stick together with a kind of "honor among thieves." (That phrase, by the way, was used as the title of an expanded universe novel in 2014.)

The world loves its own. Jesus said as much to His disciples, shortly before His betrayal, arrest, and crucifixion: "If you belonged to the world, it would love you" (John 15:19). That's not the case for Christians, though. "You do not belong to the world, but I have chosen you out of the world," Jesus said. "That is why the world hates you" (John 15:19).

If we intend to live as Christians, really submitting to God's authority and following His moral rules, we should expect opposition. Not because we're sanctimonious or obnoxious, but because Jesus' cross is an "offense" to people who don't believe (Galatians 5:11) . . . and because good lives highlight the sinfulness of others. "They are surprised that you do not join them in their reckless, wild living," the apostle Peter wrote, "and they heap abuse on you" (1 Peter 4:4).

If many of the people in Jesus' time hated Him, should we expect better treatment today? Here's a promise from the apostle Paul: "Everyone who wants to live a godly life in Christ Jesus will be persecuted" (2 Timothy 3:12).

But don't let that frighten you. Live a godly life anyway, knowing that Jesus has planned the ultimate rescue mission. Until He returns, your boldness will encourage your fellow believers (see Philippians 1:12–14), and might—just might—even change the heart of a Jabba (see verse below).

Live such good lives among the pagans that, though they accuse you of doing wrong, they may see your good deeds and glorify God on the day he visits us.

1 Peter 2:12

# HOLES IN THE FORCE

"I find your lack of faith disturbing."

**Darth Vader,** *Star Wars: A New Hope*

"MAY THE FORCE BE WITH YOU," they say in the long-ago, faraway *Star Wars* galaxy. The phrase tied for fourth place in our fan survey of favorite movie lines, along with the "I love you/I know" exchange between Princess Leia and Han Solo, and immediately after the Darth Vader quote noted above.

The Force is mysterious enough both to movie characters and moviegoers. But those of us who watch the films have a better vantage point to grasp its workings. As we do, we find some odd gaps in this "mystical energy field" as described by Han Solo.

He was not a believer. But even those who were often found the Force a tricky guide. In giving Luke Skywalker his first lessons into "a larger world," Obi-Wan Kenobi said the Force sometimes controls people and sometimes obeys their commands. Throughout the saga, the Force could give sensitive people a hint of others' presence, thoughts, and future, as well as amazing physical powers. But not every time.

When the Death Star obliterated Alderaan, Obi-Wan knew something was terribly wrong . . . but not exactly what. Even when the *Millennium Falcon* came out of hyperspace into the shattered planet's asteroid field, it would take some time for the truth to become plain.

The strange nature of the Force showed itself after Obi-Wan's death. He would occasionally return as a ghostly presence to offer wisdom to Luke . . . but even then his knowledge was incomplete. When Luke quit his Jedi training on Dagobah, Obi-Wan told Yoda, "That boy is our last hope." "No," Yoda corrected. "There is another."

Yoda had limitations, too. Often in the prequels he struggled for clarity in the Force: What were Count Dooku's real motives with the Separatists? Who ordered that clone army, supposedly for the Republic? Why were the droid foundries on Geonosis humming? "The dark side clouds everything," Yoda murmured.

Though the dark side could disrupt the Jedi's Force abilities, the Sith might also be limited. The Force's strangest failing, perhaps, occurred in *Return of the Jedi.* The Emperor, punishing Luke for his "lack of vision," shoots Force lightning into the young Jedi, who cries out to his father for help. Incredibly, Darth Vader does, tossing the maniacal Emperor into the vast power core of the Death Star. Just as incredibly, the Force does not keep the Emperor from falling to his death.

Are these limitations with the Force itself, or only with those who draw on its power? It's a good question, one that we as Christians may sometimes have in our experience with God.

Why doesn't He always come through for us? We pray for a healing, but a loved one dies. We beg for financial help but end up losing the house. We long for meaningful work but seem to be stuck in a dead-end job. Is God aware of our concerns? Does He care? Is He able to help?

The Bible character Job asked questions like those, after a series of horrific personal tragedies. "I cry out to you, God, but you do not answer. I stand up, but you merely look at me," he complained. "When I hoped for good, evil came; when I looked for light, then came darkness" (Job 30:20, 26).

God took His time before finally responding to Job—but when He did, the answers were much greater than Job's questions. In fact, God had several questions for *Job,* questions like, "Where were you when I laid the earth's foundation?" (38:4). "Do you send the lightning bolts on their way?" (39:35). "Does the eagle soar at your command?" (35:27). "Do you have an arm like God's?" (40:9).

Each and every question showed Job that God knows and controls everything—and that He knows and does what is best for us, whether we grasp that or not. Humbled, Job said to God, "Surely I spoke of things I did not understand"

(Job 42:3). There will always be holes in our understanding, as the "dark side" of sin clouds every part of our human experience. There are never holes in God's knowledge, compassion, or ability.

> Great is our Lord and mighty in power; his understanding has no limit.
>
> Psalm 147:5

# AT YOUR SERVICE

> "We seem to be made to suffer.
> It's our lot in life."
>
> **C-3PO,** *Star Wars: A New Hope*

POOR C-3PO. All he wanted to do was help, but few seemed to appreciate that.

Displaying impeccable manners and a readiness to serve, Threepio was a kind of intergalactic British butler, with an accent to match. "Fluent in over six million forms of communication," he liked to talk—but often found himself shouted down by his human companions.

"Will you shut up and listen to me?" Luke Skywalker screamed over the comlink from the Death Star's garbage masher. "Shut him up or shut him down!" Han Solo barked as Threepio tried to explain the *Millennium Falcon*'s hyper-drive problem. Even Princess Leia got into the act: "Shut *up*!" she yelled as Threepio fussed over Solo's "direct assault on an Imperial star destroyer."

At Luke's side in the Jundland Wastes, Threepio lost an arm during a Tusken raider attack. Later, in Cloud City, with the arm back in place, he was blown to pieces just as he said, "Storm troopers? Here? We're in danger . . . . I must tell the others!" What thanks did he get? Chewbacca reattaching his head backward.

From his very conception, C-3PO was meant to serve. Of course, it wasn't a human conception, as Threepio was a droid. That's a shortened form of *android,* "a mobile robot in human form." (Oddly, that term was first used in the 1750s.)

No, Threepio was conceived in the imagination of young Anakin Skywalker, who then built the machine to help his mother. C-3PO was programmed for protocol—adherence to a code of etiquette—and "human-cyborg relations." He would serve multiple generations of humans, ultimately working for Anakin's son, Luke, and his rebel compatriots.

Though Threepio was, as the official Star Wars website says, "involved in some of the galaxy's most defining moments," he never seemed to get much respect. Even in our fan survey, "Goldenrod" (to use Han Solo's nickname) earned only a combined 5 percent in the "favorite character" and "favorite non-human character" categories.

Though C-3PO had to interpret R2-D2's whistles and beeps, it was the faceless little droid who got the plum assignments—like carrying the Death Star plans or flying in Luke's X-wing. Occasionally, it seems even a kindly protocol droid can succumb to a bit of jealousy, as he once called Artoo an "overweight glob of grease!"

Many of us can probably relate. We work hard on a project at the office, and someone else gets (or worse, *steals*) the credit. We volunteer for a job at church, but the announcement of thanks somehow doesn't include our name. We do something special at home, and our spouse, or parents, or siblings don't acknowledge it. We obey the laws and pay our taxes, but it seems like those who don't are the ones who get ahead. It can be frustrating.

And yet, Jesus taught that "anyone who wants to be first must be the very last, and the servant of all" (Mark 9:35). As Jesus calmed ten "indignant" disciples, angry with James and John when their mother requested high positions in the kingdom for them, He said, "You know that the rulers of the Gentiles lord it over them . . . . Not so with you. Instead, whoever wants to become great among you must be your servant, and whoever wants to be first must be your slave—just as the Son of Man did not come to be served, but to serve" (Matthew 20:25–28). If that seems upside-down, remember that God once said, "My thoughts are not your thoughts, neither are your ways my ways" (Isaiah 55:8).

Anthony Daniels, the mime-trained actor who portrays C-3PO, didn't care for science fiction and found the original *Star Wars* script "incomprehensible." But he saw something in a concept painting of C-3PO that captured his imagination—and, ever since, his character has been the picture of faithful service.

What if people saw the same thing in us?

Serve one another humbly in love.

Galatians 5:13

"Hey, Luke—may the Force be with you."

**Han Solo,** *Star Wars: A New Hope*

BY A COMFORTABLE MARGIN, Han Solo is the "favorite character" in our fan survey. Nearly a third of all respondents identified the Harrison Ford persona as their number one choice, ahead of second-place Yoda and third-place Obi-Wan Kenobi. Of course, Han has the "cool factor" we all wish to exude. But his appeal may also lie in how similar he is to each of us.

He's a bit on the selfish side. He deals with fallout from past mistakes. He can rub people the wrong way. And he's short on cash.

Money is what brings Han Solo into the rebellion against the Empire. When Obi-Wan Kenobi and Luke Skywalker seek someone to fly them off Tatooine, Solo is the pilot they find. He demands an outrageous fee—"ten thousand, all in advance"—and Obi-Wan counters with two thousand up front, plus fifteen when they land on Alderaan. Playing it cool with his customers, Han later exults to Chewbacca, "Seventeen thousand! This could really save my neck."

He needs money to pay Jabba the Hutt for a failed smuggling run. The notorious gangster had hired out the *Millennium Falcon*, but Solo dumped his cargo before being boarded by Imperial forces. Now, in anticipation of his lost money plus a 15 percent premium, Jabba allows Han a little more time to complete his job for Luke and Obi-Wan.

The old Jedi's desire to avoid "imperial entanglements" will prove unrealistic, and Han will earn every penny of his fee during an unplanned (and undesired) visit to the Death Star. When R2-D2 discovers that Princess Leia is also there, awaiting execution, Luke urges Han to join her rescue. "They're going to kill her!" Luke says. "Better her than me," Solo grumbles.

Then Luke strikes the chord that resonates with Han: money. He mentions Leia's wealth, saying the reward for rescuing her would be almost beyond imagination. Han shoots back, "I can imagine quite a bit."  While visions of treasure dance in his head, Solo agrees to help.

He will be oil to Leia's water, human sandpaper to the smooth but equally headstrong princess and senator. But Han and company will escape the Death Star, with Leia filling a seat previously held by Obi-Wan on the *Falcon*. There, Solo clearly defines his motives: not the princess herself, not the cause, but the reward. "I'm in it for the money," he says. In disgust, Leia tells Luke, "Your friend is quite a mercenary," wondering aloud if he cares about anyone but himself.

By nature, humans are selfish. Or perhaps we should say by our *sinful* nature. Part of us—probably the lingering image of God mentioned in Genesis 1:27—longs for something better. While most of us do chase the rewards of this world, we also aspire to serve a worthwhile cause. In His mysterious and wonderful ways, God offers both.

When we understand and believe in what Jesus has done, we become His ambassadors to the world, "as though God were making his appeal through us," the apostle Paul said. What appeal? "Be reconciled to God" (2 Corinthians 5:20). There is no bigger, better cause.

And there's a remarkable reward, too. We are no longer just servants of God, we are His friends (see John 15:15) . . . and Jesus promises to *make* up whatever we *give* up for Him: "Everyone who has left houses or brothers or sisters or father or mother or wife or children or fields for my sake will receive a hundred times as much and will inherit eternal life" (Matthew 19:29).

Some preachers say that you give a dollar (to their ministry) and God gives you a hundred back. He certainly could do that . . . though it's more likely Jesus was saying you gain a worldwide network of fellow believers who will help you out in times of need. On top of that, you'll ultimately enjoy heaven—such an incredible place that gold is simply paving material (see Revelation 21:21).

We can both serve the cause and enjoy the reward. Ultimately (spoiler alert!) Han Solo did, too. Maybe that's another reason we love him.

> You make known to me the path of life; you will fill me with joy in your presence, with eternal pleasures at your right hand.
>
> Psalm 16:11

# DARK HEARTS

"Fear is the path to the dark side.
Fear leads to anger. Anger leads to hate.
Hate leads to suffering."

**Yoda,** *The Phantom Menace*

SO . . . APPARENTLY politics a long time ago in a galaxy far, far away wasn't all that different from politics here and now.

Chancellor Palpatine had every appearance of sincerity, kindliness, and wisdom. He was the very picture of determination to keep the thousand-year-old Republic from being split by the Separatists. He served as mentor to Padmé Amidala, both when she was queen and senator from Naboo, as well as to Anakin Skywalker, who always appreciated Palpatine's encouragement. "I see you becoming the greatest of all the Jedi, Anakin," the chancellor once said. "Even more powerful than Master Yoda."

But looks could be deceiving. Palpatine was nothing like his public persona.

The chancellor's heart was dark, seething, selfish; it held a lust that would stop at nothing short of galactic domination. In actuality the dark lord Darth Sidious, Palpatine lived a double life, secretly manipulating people and events toward his own desired ends.

Palpatine tried to eliminate Padmé and schemed to turn Anakin to the dark side of the Force. And the Separatist Alliance, which may have begun as a true reaction against corruption in the Republic's senate, was completely co-opted by Palpatine through his evil apprentice Count Dooku. Ultimately, the chancellor would use the Separatist "crisis" to acquire more political power and a vast clone army, ostensibly to maintain order in the galaxy. Oh, and why not also declare the Jedi enemies of the state and name himself Emperor along the way?

It was hypocrisy of the rankest sort, the kind that loves power and uses people, all the while painting itself in pretty hues of compassion. Perhaps you've noticed that in our own world?

But let's not be too tough on the politicians . . . or business leaders or media figures or whoever. At times, we *all* have dark hearts.

In the days of the early church, a sorcerer named Simon amazed the people of Samaria with his magical powers—so much so that they called him "the Great Power of God" (Acts 8:10). When Simon heard Philip preach about Jesus, though, he believed the good news and was baptized, like many of his countrymen. Simon then followed Philip, "astonished by the great signs and miracles he saw" (v. 13).

Sadly, Simon was harboring envy. When two of Jesus' main disciples came to Samaria to call the Holy Spirit upon believers, Simon wanted that power, too—and offered money to get it. Peter's response? "May your money perish with you, because you thought you could buy the gift of God with money! . . . I see that you are full of bitterness and captive to sin" (Acts 8:20, 23).

God opposes hypocrisy of *any* sort but especially the kind that claims to serve Him. Jesus came down hardest on Jewish leaders who kept other people from Him. "Woe to you, teachers of the law and Pharisees, you hypocrites!" He said that multiple times (Matthew 23:13, 15, 23, 25, 27, 29), hating that "on the outside you appear to people as righteous but on the inside you are full of hypocrisy and wickedness" (v. 28).

Some hypocrisy is blatant and intentional; sometimes it's an inner tension so common the apostle Paul calls it a law: "Although I want to do good, evil is right there with me. For in my inner being I delight in God's law; but I see another law at work in me, waging war against the law of my mind and making me a prisoner of the law of sin at work within me" (Romans 7:21–23).

Can we possibly replace hypocrisy in our hearts with integrity? Of course. As Peter told Simon, "Repent of this wickedness and pray to the Lord" (Acts 8:22). "Thanks be to God," Paul added, "who delivers me through Jesus Christ our Lord!" (Romans 7:25).

In the *Star Wars* universe, even Darth Vader—who wallowed for years in fear, anger, vengeance, and lust for power—ultimately saw the light. We who know the true "light of the world" (John 8:12) can trust Jesus to chase all the dark things from our hearts.

"I know, my God, that you test the heart and are pleased with integrity."

1 Chronicles 29:17

# UNNOTICED?

> "The more you tighten your grip,
> Tarkin, the more star systems will
> slip through your fingers."
>
> **Princess Leia,** *Star Wars: A New Hope*

IN AN ENTIRE GALAXY of star systems, there must be some overlooked, unnoticed places. There must be some overlooked, unnoticed people. After all, Chancellor Palpatine—unveiling himself to Anakin Skywalker as Darth Sidious in the *Revenge of the Sith* novel—said there were a trillion beings on the capital planet of Coruscant alone, and "in the galaxy as a whole, uncounted quadrillions." Seems like you could just disappear if you wanted to.

Or maybe not.

On the planet Naboo, as Qui-Gon Jinn warned the Gungans of an oncoming Trade Federation droid invasion, their gruff leader scoffed. Boss Nass could envision no threat to his underwater city of Otoh Gunga. "Dey not know of uss-en!"

When Qui-Gon and Obi-Wan Kenobi evacuated Queen Amidala from Naboo, they sought a quiet place to repair her damaged transport. The younger Jedi found a seemingly perfect spot in the galaxy's Outer Rim. "It's small, out of the way, poor" Obi-Wan said of Tatooine, adding, in the novelization, "it attracts little attention."

Years later, Lando Calrissian made a similar claim for his mining outpost of Cloud City, telling Han Solo and Princess Leia, "Our operation is small enough not to be noticed."

Boss Nass, Obi-Wan, and Lando were wrong.

Droid armies did know of Otoh Gunga—and they chased its inhabitants out of their homes.

Tatooine attracted all kinds of attention—from probe droids to Darth Maul to armies of storm troopers.

Darth Vader noticed Cloud City, and co-opted the place for his evil scheme to turn Luke Skywalker to the dark side.

There's no disappearing to be had, in either the *Star Wars* universe or in real life. On film, evil forces seem always to infiltrate the places where people try to hide. But that happens in our everyday experience, as well. "Our struggle is not against flesh and blood," the apostle Paul wrote to Christians in Ephesus, "but against the rulers, against the authorities, against the powers of this dark world and against the spiritual forces of evil in the heavenly realms" (Ephesians 6:12).

If the story stopped there, we'd all be miserable . . . and without hope. But happily, it's not only evil that surrounds us. In fact, the ultimate Good is at work, and there's no place in the entire universe—far beyond just our galaxy—where His children exceed His reach.

That truth astonished a songwriter of three thousand years ago. Peering into the night sky above ancient Israel, David mused, "When I consider your heavens, the work of your fingers, the moon and the stars, which you have set in place, what is mankind that you are mindful of them, human beings that you care for them?" (Psalm 8:3–4).

Though from God's perspective, "enthroned above the circle of the earth . . . its people are like grasshoppers" (Isaiah 40:22), those seemingly insignificant people are vitally important to Him. "If I go up to the heavens, you are there; if I make my bed in the depths, you are there," David wrote. "If I rise on the wings of the dawn, if I settle on the far side of the sea, even there your hand will guide me, your right hand will hold me fast" (Psalm 139:8–10).

Wherever you are, whoever you are, you are definitely noticed . . . by the all-powerful, all-loving God of the universe. He's aware of everything you experience, and He's ready to offer care, guidance, and protection—because He's always with you.

Whether you're metaphorically underwater, in a desert, or up in the clouds.

"Do not fear, for I am with you; do not be dismayed, for I am your God. I will strengthen you and help you; I will uphold you with my righteous right hand."

Isaiah 41:10

# CROSSING THE CHASM

"For luck!"

**Princess Leia,** *Star Wars: A New Hope*

LUKE AND LEIA'S dramatic escape from storm troopers on the Death Star is an iconic scene of the *Star Wars* series—and all of moviedom.

Having sprung Leia from Level 5, Detention Block AA-23—saving her from being "terminated"—Luke, Han Solo, and Chewbacca escort the princess through the corridors of the Imperial battle station, hoping to reach the *Millennium Falcon*. On the way, though, they're intercepted by a squad of storm troopers. Han shocks everyone by charging the soldiers, who turn and run the opposite direction. Chewie follows Han. Luke and Leia continue together.

Sprinting up a side hall, they burst through an open hatchway, barely stopping themselves before they pitch into a deep abyss. It's a ventilation shaft running the vertical length of the Death Star, and the catwalk across has been retracted. Princess and Jedi-to-be are stuck on a ledge about a yard square, with a good thirty feet to cross the chasm.

Fortunately for our heroes, the utility belt Luke kept from his stolen storm trooper uniform includes a cable just long and strong enough to provide an escape. Call it the "Swing to Freedom"—that's what toymaker Hasbro did with a 2002 action figure set celebrating the twenty-fifth anniversary of the film. In 2014, the Discovery Channel's *Mythbusters* show re-created the scene in real life, ultimately calling it "plausible but unlikely."

As Leia fires a blaster at oncoming storm troopers, Luke makes a perfect toss with his grappling hook, takes hold of Leia, accepts a quick kiss, and launches out over nothing. Not surprisingly, they land perfectly on the other side. The ending is happy; the chasm is crossed.

Modern translations of the Bible use the word *chasm* to describe the impassable gap between the places of reward and punishment after death. The old King James Version calls it a "great gulf." Whatever the terminology, the idea came from Jesus.

He once told the story of a wealthy man who "lived in luxury every day" while a beggar named Lazarus lay at his gate, "longing to eat what fell from the rich man's table." When each man died, angels carried Lazarus to "Abraham's side" while the rich man was tormented in Hades, terms that basically parallel *heaven* and *hell*.

The wealthy man wanted Lazarus to bring water to "cool

my tongue, because I am in agony in this fire." But Abraham told him that just wasn't possible. "Son, remember that in your lifetime you received your good things, while Lazarus received bad things, but now he is comforted here and you are in agony," Abraham said. "And besides all this, between us and you a great chasm has been set in place, so that those who want to go from here to you cannot, nor can anyone cross over from there to us" (Luke 16:19–31).

It's a disturbing picture, one that many people—even in the church—prefer not to consider. But it's hard to avoid the many disturbing things Jesus said about punishment to come (see John 5:28–29; Matthew 25:46; Mark 9:43–48).

At that same time, though, it's hard to overlook the many descriptions of God's love and His gift of salvation through the death and resurrection of Jesus Christ. Key among them, "But God demonstrates his own love for us in this: While we were still sinners, Christ died for us" (Romans 5:8), and perhaps the best-known verse in all of scripture, "For God so loved the world that he gave his one and only Son, that whoever believes in him shall not perish but have eternal life" (John 3:16).

Navigating this abyss takes not a cable but a cross. Two questions for each of us: Have I gone over the chasm myself? Am I taking anyone with me?

If you declare with your mouth, "Jesus is Lord," and believe in your heart that God raised him from the dead, you will be saved.

Romans 10:9

# WHERE DO YOU BELONG?

"You truly belong here with us
among the clouds."

**Lando Calrissian,** *The Empire Strikes Back*

IF YOU HAD TO LIVE on a Star Wars planet, which would you choose?

Probably not the volcanic Mustafar, where the climactic duel between Obi-Wan Kenobi and Anakin Skywalker occurred. Way too hot.

Probably not the storm-swept Kamino, where the locals cloned a massive, mysterious army from the bounty hunter Jango Fett. Too wet and dreary.

Probably not the overgrown Dagobah, where Yoda hid in exile after Order 66 decimated the Jedi. "A slimy mudhole," in Luke Skywalker's opinion.

Of course, those aren't places where people typically live anyway. Other planets are more suited to human life, though even they vary widely in their geography, climate, and style.

Take, for example, Tatooine, birthplace of Anakin Skywalker and the adoptive home of his son, Luke. Hot, dry, and harsh, Tatooine is populated by sturdy, hardworking folk like Luke's foster father, the moisture farmer Owen Lars.

Then there's Naboo, filled with shimmering lakes, lush plains, and cities of classic architecture. It's a perfect complement to the beautiful queen, Padmé Amidala.

We get only a brief, up-close view of Alderaan, when Bail Organa brings Padmé's baby home as his adopted daughter. The senator, his wife, and little Leia sit overlooking a mountain lake rimmed by dramatic snow-capped peaks.

Meanwhile, the "city-planet" of Coruscant is completely covered with buildings, from slender skyscrapers to the broad, five-spired Jedi temple. The galaxy's capital, with its endless lines of floating traffic, flashing video billboards, opulent theaters, and political intrigue, is the place to be if you like action. It's where the "cool kids," like Mace Windu, hang out.

In the *Star Wars* galaxy, as in real life, people like Padmé live and move in "better neighborhoods"—nicer places with more advantages and opportunities. Others, like Luke, have to climb their way out of tougher places. Still others, like Owen Lars, seem stuck in those tough places forever.

Why are we where we are? Why do some people enjoy more pleasant circumstances and better breaks? Why do others seem always to be in hard spots, living hard lives? The differences can be stark, and they affect believers as much as anyone else. (Sometimes even more so, for those Christians facing persecution around the world.)

Somehow, in His own wisdom, God has put each of us exactly where He wants us—right here, right now. In a speech to the philosophers of Athens, the apostle Paul said, "From one man [God] made all the nations, that they should inhabit the whole earth; and he marked out their appointed times in history and the boundaries of their lands" (Acts 17:26). Then within those appointed times and boundaries, God uses individuals to work out His plans. Individuals like Esther, the beautiful Jewish exile made queen of Persia. She had the chance to stop a disastrous plot against the Jews but at considerable risk to herself. "Who knows," her cousin Mordecai challenged her, "but that you have come to your royal position for such a time as this?" (Esther 4:14).

Wherever we are, whatever our resources, we should serve God as best we can. That will look different for every one of us. If you're in the place to save a nation—in the courts of Persia or Naboo—great . . . by all means do so. But if you're stuck out in the desert somewhere, that's okay, too. Do your job, live your life . . . and help out a kid who might someday change the world.

And always remember that God Himself put you where you are.

"'Well done, my good servant!' his master replied. 'Because you have been trustworthy in a very small matter, take charge of ten cities.'"

Luke 19:17

# STEALTHY ENEMIES

"Hard to see, the dark side is."

**Yoda,** *The Phantom Menace*

HUMANS LEARNED NOT TO venture far into Tatooine's Jundland Wastes. That was the domain of the Sand People, who were none too friendly to visitors.

The powerful humanoids are hideous, with bug-eyed goggles sticking through their mummy-like head wrappings. Their mouths are covered by a metallic sand filter, which distorts their already-fearsome vocalizations. (Those sounds began in real life as the braying of mules.)

No matter how nasty, the Sand People were named by a few of our survey respondents as their "favorite non-human character," putting them on the same level as C-3PO, Jabba the Hutt's rancor, and the giant asteroid worm of Episode V.

Though playing a small role in the original 1977 release, the Sand People appear in two films of the prequel trilogy. They're almost comical in *The Phantom Menace,* firing rifles at passing Pod racers. But in *Attack of the Clones,* the Sand People kidnap Anakin Skywalker's mother, Shmi, mistreating her so badly that she dies. Anakin's vengeance on the entire Sand People camp—he kills men, women, and children—is an early step in his descent to the dark side.

Anakin's stepfather, Cliegg Lars, said the Sand People "walk like men, but they're vicious, mindless monsters." He called them "Tusken Raiders," an alternative name not mentioned in Episode IV but used in the *Star Wars* novelization and Topps trading cards of the time.

The first time moviegoers learn of the creatures, Luke Skywalker is discussing the disappearance of R2-D2 with C-3PO. "Pardon me, sir, but couldn't we go after him?" Threepio asks. "It's too dangerous with all the Sand People around," Luke answers. "We'll have to wait until morning."

Morning finds the pair in the wasteland, where they catch up to Artoo. But the little droid warns of several approaching creatures. Training his macro-binoculars on some distant banthas, Luke catches sight of a Sand Person near them . . . then suddenly finds his view screen blocked by a raider directly in front of him.

That's just like the stealthy Sand People, who rode their banthas single-file to hide the size of their raiding parties. But after his silent approach, this Sand Person (identified as RR'uruurrr on StarWars.com) lets out a terrifying bellow and attacks Luke with his nasty pointed gaffi stick.

Taken completely by surprise, Luke is knocked cold in the struggle. The timely appearance of Ben Kenobi, who scares off the Sand People with his imitation of a krayt dragon call, probably saves Luke from his grandmother's fate.

Christians, too, have a stealthy enemy who would love to trap and harm us. Though Satan can never "snatch" a true follower of Jesus from God's hand (John 10:29), the devil will use any and all means to distract us—and the people we influence—from God.

Satan will often work quietly, building on the evil desires already inside us. "For out of the heart come evil thoughts," Jesus said, "murder, adultery, sexual immorality, theft, false testimony, slander. These are what defile a person" (Matthew 15:19–20; see also James 1:13–15). The devil can also sneak up on us with ideas that seem pleasant and reasonable enough but disagree with God's Word. The apostle Paul warned of people "masquerading as apostles of Christ. And no wonder, for Satan himself masquerades as an angel of light" (2 Corinthians 11:13–14).

But at some point, the enemy bellows like a Tusken Raider. "Be alert and of sober mind," the apostle Peter wrote. "Your enemy the devil prowls around like a roaring lion looking for someone to devour" (1 Peter 5:8). When does a lion roar? According to the prophet Amos, not until he locks on to his prey (3:4).

So how do *we* avoid that locked-on roar?

Only through God's Word. The Bible is both the radar that alerts us to Satan's approach and the weapon we use to blast him. It was Jesus' answer to three temptations in the desert (see Matthew 4:1–11). It is "like fire . . . like a hammer that breaks a rock in pieces" (Jeremiah 23:29).

As Christians, we have a stealthy enemy, but through Scripture, we know just how he operates. Will we act on that knowledge?

> . . . in order that Satan might not outwit us. For we are not unaware of his schemes.
>
> 2 Corinthians 2:11

# GOING BACK, GOING FORWARD

"I don't trust Lando."

**Princess Leia,** *The Empire Strikes Back*

HAN SOLO AND LANDO CALRISSIAN go way back. But time doesn't always translate to trust.

A gambler and all-around scoundrel, Lando was running a tibanna gas mine—above the planet Bespin, under the Empire's radar—when Han came calling. The *Millennium Falcon,* once Lando's pride and joy, needed hyperdrive repairs if Han and Leia were to evade Darth Vader and rejoin the rebellion.

"Can you trust him?" Leia asked. "No," Han replied. But with few real alternatives, he set course for Cloud City.

In Lando's airspace, the *Falcon* got a chilly reception from laser-firing escorts. Han's radio name-dropping—"I'm trying to reach Lando Calrissian"—didn't help. Chewbacca's grunted question took Han aback. "That was a long time ago," he said. "I'm sure he's forgotten about that."

Or maybe not. After receiving permission to land on Platform 327, Han exited the *Falcon* and walked tentatively down the ramp. Lando, followed by a few stone-faced aides, marched up muttering, "You slimy, double-crossing, no-good swindler . . . you've got a lot of guts coming here after what you pulled."

Han's eyes widened at Lando's words, and at the quick lunge that became a hug. Now smiling and laughing, Lando welcomed the "old pirate" with a "Good to see you!" When Han requested repairs for the *Falcon,* we learned something of the men's history. "What have you done to my ship?" Lando cried. "Your ship?" Han countered. "Remember . . . you lost her to me fair and square."

The *Falcon* was forgotten when Leia appeared. Lando was clearly smitten. She definitely was not, telling Han shortly afterward, "I don't trust Lando."

Woman's intuition proved true as Leia, Han, and Chewie walked to a Cloud City dining hall for refreshment. "I've just made a deal that will keep the Empire out of here forever," Lando said, opening the door to reveal . . . Darth Vader.

"I had no choice," Lando said flatly. "They arrived right before you did. I'm sorry." In following scenes, he suffered the slings and arrows of his offended guests. "You fixed us all real good, didn't you?" Han growled. "Do you think that after what you did to Han, we're going to trust you?" Leia railed.

Turns out Lando *was* speaking truth: He had been at Vader's mercy, and he was honestly sorry. Lando would endanger himself to make good, ultimately becoming a hero. But his reputation for shadiness nearly derailed him—especially when Chewbacca, furious over the carbon-freezing of Han, almost choked Lando to death.

He's only a movie character, but Lando's ethics have real-life parallels. In the book of Genesis, Jacob—younger twin of Esau—manipulated his brother for personal gain. Esau dreamed of vengeance (see Genesis 27).

Jacob was God's choice to head the "great nation" promised to the boys' grandfather Abraham (Genesis 12:2). That was against custom, though, as older brothers always took family leadership. Jacob took matters into his own hands, cheating Esau of his firstborn benefits. "Isn't he rightly named Jacob?" Esau cried, referring to the meaning of the name: *deceiver.* "This is the second time he has taken advantage of me: He took my birthright, and now he's taken my blessing!" (Genesis 27:36).

Esau eventually mellowed. Years later, he reconciled with Jacob, who approached his brother in terror (see Genesis 32–33). God was still using Jacob to accomplish His plans . . . but often despite, not because of, Jacob's behavior.

So what about us? With family, friends, coworkers, and acquaintances, is our word reliable? Our motives unquestionable? King Solomon wrote that relationships come down to love and faithfulness. "Bind them around your neck, write them on the tablet of your heart. Then you will win favor and a good name in the sight of God and man" (Proverbs 3:3–4).

Ideally, by living honorable lives, we never give up our favor and good name. But since we're only human, and susceptible to the pursuit of our own interests at the expense of others, what can we do after we've pulled a Jacob or a Lando?

The Bible offers no guaranteed, multi-step plan, but it seems any hope of restoring broken relationships starts with the humility Jacob showed to Esau. In the custom of the time, the younger brother bowed before his elder—not just once, but seven times—and all of his servants, wives, and children did the same (Genesis 33:3, 6–7). The great apostle Paul humbled himself after speaking sharply to the high priest, who most of us would probably think deserved a good smackdown (see Acts 23:1–5).

After we admit our wrongdoing, all we can do is live and love consistently, treating others the way we'd want to be treated ourselves (Matthew 7:12).

And pray that God will ultimately restore our good name and trust with others.

> Be careful to do what is right in the eyes of everyone. If it is possible, as far as it depends on you, live at peace with everyone.
>
> Romans 12:17–18

# I HEAR VOICES

"Mind what you have learned. Save you it can."

**Yoda,** *The Empire Strikes Back*

EVERYONE, IT SEEMED, wanted Luke Skywalker's ear.

Uncle Owen either barked out orders or begged Luke's help, depending on the day. Newly purchased from the Jawas, C-3PO kept up a barrage of questions and commentary. Han Solo cautiously probed Luke's thoughts on Princess Leia: "You think a princess and a guy like me—" Luke's quick *no* brought an end to that conversation.

The Jedi master Yoda taught, shamed, and cajoled Luke. Darth Vader shared the shocking news that he was Luke's father—then urged the young man to join him on the dark side, suggesting they could rule the galaxy as father and son. The emperor coaxed Luke, over and over again, to give in to his aggression and hatred.

Ben Kenobi urged Luke to learn the ways of the Force, join him on a trip to Alderaan, and be part of the "idealistic crusade" his Uncle Owen had long feared. After the Empire murdered Luke's aunt and uncle, pushing him into the rebel camp, Luke regularly heard Obi-Wan's encouragement and instruction . . . which continued even beyond the old Jedi's death in a lightsaber battle.

In the climactic moments of Episode IV, as Luke's X-wing flashes toward its target on the Death Star, Obi-Wan speaks. "Use the Force, Luke," the disembodied voice murmurs. Confused, Luke looks away briefly, seeming to question if he had actually heard something. But when Obi-Wan speaks again—"Let go, Luke"—the young hero switches off his targeting computer, relies on the Force, and fires his photon torpedoes into the exhaust port bull's-eye.

Obi-Wan's voice—along with the last-second reappearance of Han Solo in the *Millennium Falcon*—had saved the day. As the surviving pilots return to the rebel base, Obi-Wan speaks to Luke again: "Remember, the Force will be with you always."

At times, we all need some affirmation and guidance. It would be great to have that in an authoritative, audible voice like Obi-Wan Kenobi's. God, however, tends to speak to Christians in different ways.

In the Bible, He did sometimes talk directly with people. "The LORD would speak to Moses face to face, as one speaks to a friend" (Exodus 33:11), and Jesus, after His ascension to heaven, got a proud Pharisee's attention by shining a bright light and asking, "Saul, Saul, why do you persecute me?" (Acts 9:4).

Certainly, God can speak audibly today if He chooses to. And He can communicate as He did with the founding father of the Jews: "The word of the LORD came to Abram in a vision: 'Do not be afraid, Abram. I am your shield, your very great reward'" (Genesis 15:1).

But it's more likely that God will "speak" to us through our thoughts and feelings. "My conscience is clear," the apostle Paul (the former persecutor Saul) said, because "it is the Lord who judges me" (1 Corinthians 4:4). And Jesus mentioned the primary channel God uses to communicate His thoughts and desires: "The [Holy] Spirit will receive from me what he will make known to you" (John 16:15).

Of course, there's one more way God speaks, and it's the way that validates any other message we believe we've heard: the Bible. Because our hearts and minds are still vulnerable to selfishness and sin, God gave us His Word as a perfect, unchanging guide. We can listen for God's voice—in our own spirit, or through friends, preachers, or media—then compare what we hear against Scripture. "Consult God's instruction and the testimony of warning," the prophet Isaiah said. "If anyone does not speak according to this word, they have no light of dawn" (Isaiah 8:20).

God's voice may never be as clear to us as Obi-Wan's was to Luke. But if we keep our ears tuned for God's "gentle whisper" (1 Kings 19:12) and confirm what we hear by God's Word, we will know exactly what He wants us to know.

Now the Berean Jews were of more noble character than those in Thessalonica, for they received the message with great eagerness and examined the Scriptures every day to see if what Paul said was true.

Acts 17:11

# BOBA'S FATE

> "He's no good to me dead."
>
> **Boba Fett,** *The Empire Strikes Back*

SO, WHAT DID YOU THINK of Boba Fett's demise?

Our fan survey found more than a fifth of respondents thought it was "really disappointing," while a similar number felt it was "kind of dumb." To be fair, almost equal numbers either "loved it" or believed "it was okay."

A menacing figure in battered gray and green armor, Boba Fett first appeared in Episode V, *The Empire Strikes Back,* though George Lucas later inserted him into a scene of the 1997 special edition of Episode IV. Of several bounty hunters assembled by Darth Vader to capture Han Solo, he's the most ruthless and cunning.

At least, we think so. Boba Fett has only a handful of scenes and lines in the original trilogy. We're left to assume he's fierce by the looks of his slit-eyed helmet, by his bristling weaponry and gadgets, and by a command Vader specifically directs to him: "No disintegrations!"

It's Boba Fett, in his odd ship *Slave 1,* who tails Han Solo to Cloud City, then carries the carbon-encased pilot back to

Jabba the Hutt's palace on Tatooine. In those desert wastes, the fearsome bounty hunter will meet a comical end.

In *Return of the Jedi,* Luke and Leia have both made their way to Jabba's lair to try to rescue Han. Leia succeeds in unfreezing him, but she's captured and chained to Jabba as a kind of Huttese eye candy. Luke survives his drop into the rancor's pit, but when he kills the horrible beast, Jabba is furious.

In the Dune Sea, at the Pit of Carkoon, Luke and Han will be forced to walk the plank and drop into the mouth of a creature called the Sarlacc. In its belly, as C-3PO interprets Jabba's pronouncement, they will be "slowly digested over one thousand years." But then Luke does a nifty flip off the plank, R2-D2 shoots him his lightsaber, and a battle ensues.

Boba Fett joins in the melee, zooming from Jabba's sail barge to the skiff holding Luke and Han. He's aiming for Luke when Chewbacca barks out a warning—and Han, still recovering from his carbon-blindness, whirls around saying "Boba Fett? Where?" Han accidentally bumps the bounty hunter's jetpack, igniting the rockets and shooting Boba into the side of Jabba's barge. He bounces off, tumbling down the pit and into the Sarlacc's mouth.

Boba was gone, and many filmgoers said, "Really?"

Fans of the expanded universe point out that Boba Fett escaped the Sarlacc to star in later stories . . . but his movie history ends with the Sarlacc's silly burp. Even George Lucas, in the audio commentary to Episode VI, admitted that, in light of Boba Fett's ultimate popularity, it was "a misstep that we wouldn't make more of the event of his defeat."

When we watch movies, most of us want a "satisfying" end for the bad guy—namely, that he pays in full measure for his misdeeds. It's a natural reaction but not a *super*-natural one. God prefers to give sinners every possible chance to come clean. He told the prophet Ezekiel, "As surely as I live, declares the Sovereign LORD, I take no pleasure in the death of the wicked, but rather that they turn from their ways and live. Turn! Turn from your evil ways!" (Ezekiel 33:11).

But it's not only the Boba Fetts of the world who need God's kindness—in reality, we're *all* bad guys. "All have turned away, all have become corrupt," King David wrote. "There is no one who does good, not even one" (Psalm 14:3). And the worst thing about human corruption is that "the wages of sin is death" (Romans 6:23).

Still, in His mercy and grace, God "is patient with you, not wanting anyone to perish, but everyone to come to repentance" (2 Peter 3:9). Jesus proved that in His last moments on the cross, welcoming the thief at His side into "paradise" (Luke 23:43). Saving souls was the whole point of Jesus' ministry on earth, whether He was pursuing each one of us as a lost sheep, a lost coin, or a lost son (see Luke

15). "The Son of Man came," Jesus said, using a prophetic term for himself, "to seek and to save the lost" (Luke 19:10).

Thanks to the love of God the Father and the sacrifice of His Son, Jesus Christ, humanity's fate—spiritual death—is completely avoidable.

Digest that truth for awhile.

> The gift of God is eternal life in Christ Jesus our Lord.
>
> Romans 6:23

# A SMALL VULNERABILITY

> "If the Rebels have obtained a complete
> technical readout of this station, it is possible,
> however unlikely, that they might find
> a weakness and exploit it."
>
> **General Tagge,** *Star Wars: A New Hope*

IT SEEMED INVINCIBLE. We all know the story well enough, though, to recognize the vulnerability of the Death Star.

Getting mentions from many of our fan survey respondents, as both the "favorite mechanical device" and "favorite locale" of the *Star Wars* series, the Death Star was the Empire's ultimate weapon. But it takes a lot of time and thought to create a battle station the size of a moon with the firepower to obliterate a planet. So in the latter days of the galactic Republic, with the Empire still a dream in the evil heart of Chancellor Palpatine, he secretly worked with the Geonosians to develop plans for the metallic menace.

Geonosians were bug-like creatures, ugly and energetic. On their rocky, desert planet, foundries and factories cranked out the droid armies of the Separatist Alliance that fought the Republic's troopers in the Clone Wars. Palpatine

118 • PAUL KENT

had manipulated both sides, engineering the war as a way to eliminate the Jedi and take command of the galaxy.

The Geonosian leader, Poggle the Lesser, would soon find that alliances with Palpatine were one-sided. After the chancellor received the Death Star plans, Palpatine—also known as Darth Sidious—ordered his apprentice Darth Vader to kill Poggle and leaders of the anti-Republic forces.

Twenty years later, the Emperor and Vader presided over a complete and operational Death Star, which proved its destructive power by blasting Princess Leia's home planet of Alderaan to rubble. But Leia, who lost her adoptive father, Senator Bail Organa, in the blast, had somehow acquired the plans to the Death Star and sent them to Obi-Wan Kenobi by way of R2-D2. The computer readouts would show the one small vulnerability that would allow Luke Skywalker to blow the massive weapon out of space.

It was a thermal exhaust port, less than two meters wide, connected to the space station's main power reactor. Because the Death Star defenses were designed for a full-scale assault, rebel analysts had determined an attack by small, single-pilot fighters could possibly succeed. *If* they could get by the station's outer protections, *if* they could avoid the surface-mounted laser cannons, *if* they could outrace the Empire's TIE fighters, *if* someone could launch a photon torpedo into that little opening . . . then the invincible Death Star would prove conquerable after all. And that's exactly what happened.

The Grand Moff Tarkin and the Emperor, focusing on their battle station's power while ignoring its vulnerability, exemplified the truth of Proverbs 16:18—"Pride goes before destruction, a haughty spirit before a fall."

In everyday life, our own vulnerabilities can lead to major explosions. The temptations we each face, which vary from person to person, are "little foxes that ruin the vineyards" (Song 2:15). If we don't deal with them properly, we might find ourselves in a place we never dreamed we'd be.

The Bible's Samson is an extreme example. Specially called by God to be a judge (or "deliverer") of Israel, Samson was given incredible physical strength for battle. But his hunger for women—even of the enemy Philistines—led to a humiliating downfall (see Judges 16:1–21).

Sexual temptations are a huge vulnerability for many but by no means the only kind. In the Ten Commandments (Exodus 20:1–17), God warns against "big sins" like adultery and murder but also prohibits stealing. Few of us would ever rob a bank . . . but would we waste time on the job, download files we haven't paid for, even "borrow" money without asking to get out of a tight spot? The tenth commandment says, "You shall not covet," which means we can't even *want* the things other people have. That's a seemingly small vulnerability . . . but one that can still lead to big problems.

Like the Death Star, none of us is invincible. What is your "exhaust port," the potential entry point for temptation and trouble? What can you do to seal it off?

> Above all else, guard your heart, for everything you do flows from it.
>
> Proverbs 4:23

# "CAN YOU SPEAK BOCCE?"

> "R2-Dee Toa. C-3POA.
> Ay tuta mishka Jabba du Hutt?
> Kuja wanki mitby cosa."
>
> **C-3PO,** *Return of the Jedi*

OF COURSE C-3PO could speak Bocce. He was quick to remind everyone that he was fluent in over six million forms of communication. The real question was this: Why did Luke Skywalker's aunt need a Bocce translator?

It was Luke's aunt, Beru Lars, who introduced moviegoers to the hero of Episodes IV, V, and VI. The young moisture farmer and future Jedi knight had just made his on-screen debut, preparing to review the Jawas' collection of second-hand droids when Beru called, "Luke!" She wanted her nephew to remind his uncle Owen, "If he gets a translator, be sure it speaks Bocce."

This, and Owen's question to Threepio outside the Jawas' sand crawler ("Can you speak Bocce?") are the only "canonical" references to the language. But our friends at Wookieepedia have distilled this definition from expanded universe lore: Bocce is "an interplanetary trade language

. . . not commonly used by most." They even provide some helpful terms, if you'd like to use them on unsuspecting friends: *Keezx* (yes). *Nokeezx* (no). *Koo-loozi* (good day).

The mystery of Beru's request notwithstanding, C-3PO was prepared to assist with every linguistic need. He clarified R2-D2's whistles and beeps for human comprehension; served as interpreter, however reluctantly, in Jabba the Hutt's court; and held Ewoks spellbound with the story of the rebellion, using their own language plus sound effects. C-3PO even discerned the nature of a weak, static-filled signal picked up by rebel radio operators on Hoth. "This signal is not used by the Alliance," he reported. "It could be an Imperial code."

Throughout the saga, Threepio's language skills proved indispensable, as he ensured that those around him were "in the know." We as Christians have a similar duty.

One of the first signs of the Holy Spirit's arrival on earth was the ability of first-century Christians to speak in other languages. It happened as "God-fearing Jews from every nation under heaven" gathered in Jerusalem to celebrate Pentecost. "Aren't all these who are speaking Galileans?" the visitors asked. "Then how is it that each of us hears them in our native language?" (Acts 2:5, 7–8).

Well, it was a miracle . . . one that God used to kick-start the church, which grew from 120 to more than three thousand that day (see Acts 1:15, 2:41). But in every time and place, God calls His people to "speak the language" of others, to ensure that they understand the good news of salvation through Christ.

Jesus Himself set the example. "With many similar parables Jesus spoke the word to them, as much as they could understand," the Gospel writer Mark noted. "He did not say anything to them without using a parable" (Mark 4:33–34).

The apostle Paul followed suit, tailoring his message to his audience's style and understanding. To immature Christians in Corinth, "I gave you milk, not solid food, for you were not yet ready for it" (1 Corinthians 3:2). To the Greek thinkers in Athens, he gave a deep philosophical speech (see Acts 17:16–34).

Over the centuries, Christians have learned other languages to translate Scripture—sometimes *creating* written languages for those cultures that lacked one. Many have shared the story of Jesus through art, from sculptures and paintings, to the passion play at Oberammergau, Germany, to Handel's *Messiah*. Many have used the media—books, radio, television, movies, the internet—to send the gospel to people wherever they are.

Theologians would call that "contextualizing" the message, and it's something that every one of us can do. We don't have to be philosophers or filmmakers or linguists.

We don't even have to be fluent in our own language! We just need to care about others, and know them well enough to share the truth in an effective way.

Koo-loozi.

> I have become all things to all people so that by all possible means I might save some.
>
> 1 Corinthians 9:22

# FROZEN IN CARBONITE

> "Train yourself to let go
> of everything you fear to lose."
>
> **Yoda,** *Revenge of the Sith*

DARING, HANDSOME, quick with a wisecrack, Han Solo represents the perfect film character. Women want to be with him; men want to be him.

But even an idealized movie hunk can find that his luck runs out.

After botching a smuggling run for the Tatooine gangster Jabba the Hutt, Han found a price on his head—and bounty hunters on his tail. He was able to dispatch the bug-eyed Greedo in the Mos Eisley cantina, but at Cloud City, Boba Fett proved too tough to elude.

Truth be told, Boba had a huge assist from Darth Vader, who engineered Solo's capture to lure Luke Skywalker. Knowing that Luke's Force-sensitivity would alert him to the suffering of Han and Princess Leia, Vader dangled them as bait. And, disregarding the warnings of Yoda on Dagobah, Luke bit—quickly piloting his X-wing toward his friends.

High above the planet Bespin, Vader advanced a plan to capture Luke, present him to the Emperor, and turn the young Jedi to the dark side. Skywalker would be frozen in carbonite for the journey . . . but in a moment of caution, Vader decided to test the process on Boba Fett's prize.

Solo was being crushed by the heaviest powers in the galaxy: the most notorious bounty hunter . . . the most unscrupulous gangster . . . the most fearsome Sith lord . . . even, by extension, the most evil emperor. Soon, as Leia and Chewbacca watched in despair, Han was lowered into a freezing chamber for what could be the cocky pilot's final journey.

Encased in a block of carbonite—"he should be quite well protected . . . if he survived the freezing process, that is," offered the ever-helpful C-3PO—Solo was removed from the pit by an overhead crane. Nasty little Ugnaughts pushed on the block till it fell heavily to the horizontal. Then city administrator Lando Calrissian checked Han's vital signs and murmured the words his friends longed to hear: "He's alive."

Han had survived the ordeal, but—encased in metal and set for delivery to Jabba—he was not doing well.

Maybe you can relate. If not now, someday you will.

At times, it seems as if every power in life weighs against us. We feel trapped, stuck in a tight spot that barely allows us to breathe. Our circumstances are paralyzing, and—like Han Solo—if someone gave us the slightest push, we'd topple to the ground with a depressing clang. We're alive, but the future looks grim.

Maybe your family and friends are gone, or you have an unfulfilled longing, or you don't like where God is leading you. If so, you're in good—actually, biblical—company:

David—already running for his life from King Saul—once found his home city burned by enemy raiders, with his and his men's families kidnapped. Even worse, "the men were talking of stoning him" (1 Samuel 30:6).

Hannah—childless, with a polygamous husband—was provoked by her fertile rival Peninnah "till she wept and would not eat" (1 Samuel 1:7).

Jonah—tapped as prophet to the vicious Assyrians—tried to evade God's call but wound up inside a giant fish (Jonah 1:17).

What's the way out of *that* carbonite?

The answer is simple in theory but tough in practice: pray. Talk to God, even when you don't feel like it . . . especially then. "David found strength in the LORD his God" (1 Samuel 30:6). Hannah said, "I am a woman who is deeply troubled . . . . I have been praying here out of my great anguish and grief" (1 Samuel 1:15–16). Underwater, Jonah prayed, "In my distress I called to the LORD, and he answered me" (Jonah 2:2).

God hears prayers, even those that aren't pretty. So pray. The answer may not be immediate—Han wasn't rescued till the next movie—but better times are ahead.

Even if not on this planet.

Do not be anxious about anything, but in every situation, by prayer and petition, with thanksgiving, present your requests to God.

Philippians 4:6

# PODRACING

"You must have Jedi reflexes if you race pods."

**Qui-Gon Jinn,** *The Phantom Menace*

NINE-YEAR-OLD Anakin Skywalker, destined to become "the best star pilot in the galaxy" in Obi-Wan Kenobi's opinion, had an appetite for adventure. He fed on the dangerous sport of Podracing.

A mechanical prodigy, Anakin had secretly built his own racer under the ample nose of Mos Espa junk dealer Watto, who owned the boy and his mother as slaves. Of unusual instinct and reflex, Anakin was the only human able to race pods—many drivers had more than two eyes or arms or some other physical advantage.

It was this Podracing ability that first caught Qui-Gon Jinn's attention. Trapped on Tatooine with the crippled starship of Naboo's Princess Amidala, the Jedi master found himself in the home of Anakin's mother, Shmi. To her chagrin, the boy boasted of his talents. Qui-Gon replied, "You must have Jedi reflexes if you race pods."

His perception was correct—Anakin would later learn

Jedi ways under Obi-Wan—but in the short term, the young-ster's racing abilities offered Qui-Gon, Obi-Wan, and Padmé their only hope of escaping the desert planet.

Sensing that the Force might help Anakin win the big Boonta Eve Podrace two days hence, Qui-Gon played on Watto's known weakness for gambling. The junk dealer could have the queen's spaceship unless Anakin finished first—in which case Qui-Gon would get his repair parts . . . and Anakin his freedom.

So, with even greater passion, the boy raced. His odd machine—a pair of jet engines connected by a sizzling "energy binder" and pulling Anakin's pod by steel cables—careened over the landscape like a lightning bolt late for a date. Against racers from "all corners of the Outer Rim territories"—Ben Quadinaros, Ody Mandrell, and the win-at-all-costs Sebulba, among others—Anakin twisted and turned, climbed and plunged, anticipated and fended off surprises both random and of evil intent. Throw in a few Tusken Raiders taking potshots, and the Podrace becomes a good metaphor for life.

Some lives feature more twists and turns than others . . . some have more hills and others more valleys . . . but every life passes quickly. Days may be long, but years are short—and they only pick up speed as they go. Life flashes by like a Podracer—as the biblical Job said, "my days are swifter than a runner . . . like eagles swooping down on their prey" (Job 9:25–26).

If you're old enough to have seen *Star Wars* in its first release, consider that that's been over thirty-eight years ago! If you're a younger fan, and have yet to sense the snowballing nature of time . . . you will. Whatever your age, recognizing the brevity of life is the first step toward making the most of it.

"Show me, LORD, my life's end and the number of my days," the psalm writer David prayed. "You have made my days a mere handbreadth; the span of my years is as nothing before you" (Psalm 39:4–5). Job, who experienced crushing losses, saw both the speed and sorrow of life: "Mortals, born of woman, are of few days and full of trouble. They spring up like flowers and wither away; like fleeting shadows, they do not endure" (Job 14:1–2).

Job lived to be 140 (Job 42:16). David, who lived half that long (2 Samuel 5:4), echoed Job's thoughts: "Everyone is but a breath, even those who seem secure. Surely everyone goes around like a mere phantom; in vain they rush about, heaping up wealth without knowing whose it will finally be" (Psalm 39:5-6).

What's the answer to a life that's too fast and often disappointing? Remember God. The very next thing David said was, "Lord, what do I look for? My hope is in you" (v. 7).

Remember your Creator in the days of your youth, before the days of trouble come and the years approach when you will say, "I find no pleasure in them."

Ecclesiastes 12:1

# JUDGING YODA

"Judge me by my size, do you?"

**Yoda,** *The Empire Strikes Back*

LUKE SKYWALKER had a poor first impression of Yoda.

The Force and Jedi knighthood were fresh concepts when Luke crashed his X-wing into a Dagobah swamp. A ghostly Obi-Wan had told Luke to visit the star system for training by Yoda; from his perch in the back of Luke's starfighter, R2-D2 suggested avoiding the place altogether. For awhile in the swamp, Luke's body language said he wished he'd listened to Artoo.

The aspiring Jedi thought the dank, snake-infested swamp was creepy, especially when he sensed he was being watched. Whirling with his blaster, Luke found the observer to be harmless enough—a green humanoid all of two feet tall.

Speaking with odd syntax and plenty of "heh's" and "hmm's," the tiny creature was voiced by six-foot, two-inch Englishman Frank Oz, who also portrayed the Muppets' Miss Piggy and Fozzie Bear. To *Star Wars* fans, though, Oz is plain and simply Yoda.

The master himself had found Luke, a fact that completely escaped the impatient visitor—especially as Yoda toyed and dallied to gauge Luke's Jedi potential. The would-be pupil failed the test, assuming the chatty, nosy creature was an obstacle to his goal. Actually, the little swamp dweller *was* the goal.

At first glance, there wasn't much to Yoda. "Judge me by my size, do you?" he asked, before lifting Luke's sunken X-wing with the Force. Luke was there only because of Obi-Wan, who'd prevailed upon Yoda from the great beyond. Having heard Ben's voice and realizing just who he'd met, Luke scrambled to overcome the disrespect he had shown.

We humans often judge quickly, then need to amend our words and attitudes toward others. Our assumptions based on others' appearance or social status or unspoken beliefs can miss the mark—sometimes badly. That's why Jesus said, "Stop judging by mere appearances, but instead judge correctly" (John 7:24).

In His day, many dismissed Jesus Himself. "He had no beauty or majesty to attract us," Isaiah prophesied centuries before. "He was despised and rejected by mankind . . . we held him in low esteem" (Isaiah 53:2–3). The people of Nazareth, Jesus' hometown, judged like that. "'Where did this man get this wisdom and these miraculous powers?' they asked. 'Isn't this the carpenter's son?' . . . They took offense at him" (Matthew 13:54–55, 57). Clearly, they judged poorly.

Even many who don't claim to follow Jesus can quote His famous rule, "Do not judge, or you too will be judged"

(Matthew 7:1). Those words certainly apply to the condescending attitudes like those of His hometown Nazarenes, as well as our own hypocritical moments when we want to point out small sins in others as we commit big sins ourselves (Matthew 7:3–5).

But Jesus never said "anything goes." He was perfectly willing to judge people's *behavior* in the light of God's moral commands as found in Scripture. "Do not think that I have come to abolish the Law or the Prophets," He said in Matthew 5:17, referring to key sections of the Old Testament. And, though He refused to condemn a woman caught in the act of adultery, Jesus did tell her, "Go now and leave your life of sin" (John 8:11).

So, judge me by my size, do you? No. Judge my behavior in the light of God's Word? Yes . . . but with grace, please.

> But the LORD said to Samuel, "Do not consider his appearance or his height, for I have rejected him. The LORD does not look at the things people look at. People look at the outward appearance, but the LORD looks at the heart."
>
> 1 Samuel 16:7

# WHAT THEY WANTED TO HEAR

"Once more, the Sith will rule the galaxy.
And we shall have . . . peace."

**Emperor Palpatine,** *Revenge of the Sith*

SO HOW DO YOU become dictator of an entire galaxy?

If you're Emperor Palpatine, you start with flattery and deception—generally, telling people just what they want to hear.

As mentor to the young Queen Amidala of Naboo, Senator Palpatine seemed exactly the wise and experienced leader needed to manage the crisis of the Trade Federation invasion. But we learn later that Palpatine himself—as the evil Sith lord Darth Sidious—actually initiated the conflict.

Early on, as the senate argued over a response, Palpatine quietly suggested the no-confidence vote in Chancellor Valorum that led to his own chancellorship. Later, having gained additional powers but needing even more author-ity to use the clone army he'd secretly arranged, Palpatine orchestrated an assassination attempt on now-senator Amidala, shuttled her out of the capital for "safety," and casually manipulated her replacement.

"What senator would have the *courage* to propose such a radical amendment?" he mused, while discussing an emergency powers act with several politicians. The lingering shot of Naboo's acting senator, Jar Jar Binks, indicated exactly what was to come: "Senators, dellow felegates . . . mesa propose that the senate give immediately emergency powers to the supreme chancellor."

There was applause for Jar Jar's motion, as there was for Palpatine's speech accepting the unprecedented authority. "It is with great reluctance that I have agreed to this calling," he intoned. "I love democracy. I love the Republic. The power you give me I will lay down when this crisis has abated."

Or maybe not. The chancellor continued to deceive the senate, solidifying his hold on power as he also maneuvered Anakin Skywalker toward the dark side. Palpatine had long flattered Anakin, telling the young man he was the most gifted Jedi he'd ever seen—and would become the most powerful. Then, as Anakin wrestled with terrifying nightmares of his beloved Padmé's death, Palpatine knew exactly what to say.

It was a story, a Sith legend of a certain Darth Plagueis the Wise. "He had such a knowledge of the dark side," Palpatine almost purred, "he could even keep the ones he cared about from dying." The story stirred hope in Anakin's heart and, combined with Palpatine's deceitful discrediting of the Jedi council, pushed "the chosen one" into the realm of the Sith.

Now, with a powerful apprentice to support him, Palpatine elevated his aggression. He sent Anakin, with the new name "Darth Vader," to empty the Jedi temple and commanded clone troopers to execute Order 66, the wholesale slaughter of the Jedi dispersed to battle zones. In time, those troopers—supposedly amassed to protect the galaxy—would subjugate it as Imperial stormtroopers. Of course, Palpatine described it differently: "In order to ensure security and continuing stability, the Republic will be reorganized into the first Galactic Empire!" he proclaimed to a cheering senate. "For a safe and secure society."

If the Force is the God figure of the *Star Wars* universe, Emperor Palpatine must be the devil. Jesus once said of Satan, "there is no truth in him. When he lies, he speaks his native language, for he is a liar and the father of lies" (John 8:44). Over thousands of years of human history, Satan has spread his deception, with the ultimate goal of keeping people from God.

Tragically, many believe the lies. They reject Jesus, who called Himself "the way and the truth and the life" (John 14:6). But even those of us who know Jesus can find ourselves pulled, like an Anakin, toward the false claims of Satan. He dangles every imaginable temptation before us, hoping to turn us from God's narrow road that leads to life (Matthew 7:14).

Centuries before Jesus, the prophet Isaiah had warned of a time when people would "call evil good and good evil" (Isaiah 5:20). That's an apt description of Palpatine—as well as many people today. With an upside-down view of reality, they're like the galactic senators cheering the Sith lord's usurpation. "So this is how liberty dies," Padme muttered.

Jesus said, "The truth will set you free" (John 8:32). And He asked His Father to "sanctify," or set apart, His followers "by the truth; your word is truth" (John 17:17). Jesus Himself is the Word (John 1:1), and we know Him through God's written word, the Bible.

So the apostle Paul urged Timothy (and all of us) to "continue in what you have learned and have become convinced of . . . the Holy Scriptures, which are able to make you wise for salvation through faith in Christ Jesus" (2 Timothy 3:14–15).

That's just what we *need* to hear.

> Turn my eyes away from worthless things; preserve my life according to your word.
>
> PSALM 119:37

# NOOOOOOO!

"I am your father."

**Darth Vader**, *The Empire Strikes Back*

IN A LIGHTSABER BATTLE on Cloud City, Luke Skywalker got his hand cut off and, figuratively, his heart ripped out. You probably know the story, but here's the background:

As if on a giant, three-dimensional graph, the galaxy's most important lines have converged at one tiny point: Lando Calrissian's mining outpost high above the planet Bespin. Han Solo and Princess Leia (along with Chewbacca and C-3PO) escape the Rebel base on Hoth just ahead of Darth Vader. He assembles bounty hunters, including Boba Fett, in a plan to capture Han and Leia to lure his true prey, Luke Skywalker.

It seems bounty hunters won't be necessary when Imperial scouts see the *Millennium Falcon* emerge from hiding in an asteroid field. The woefully outgunned ship with a broken hyperdrive is doomed but for Han's quick thinking, which impresses even the skeptical Leia. His out-with-the-garbage trick fools the crew of Vader's star destroyer . . . but Boba Fett, in his ship *Slave 1,* surreptitiously tails the *Falcon* as it makes for Cloud City and repairs.

Before Han and Leia reach Lando's outpost, Boba tips off Vader. Now the trap is set for Luke, who dutifully plots a straight line from the swamps of Dagobah.

Soon, with Han frozen in carbonite and Leia, Chewbacca, and C-3PO in custody, Vader turns his attention to Luke, who arrives with blaster, lightsaber, and perhaps too much confidence in his unfinished Jedi training.

The two rivals—with a shocking, soon-to-be-disclosed secret—duel in a control room overlooking an immense cylindrical shaft. The novelization of *The Empire Strikes Back* describes the breathtaking setting as a part of Cloud City's power reactor.

Vader plays dirty, using the Force's dark side to hurl equipment at his opponent. Battered, Luke is sucked into the reactor shaft when a large hunk of machinery breaks through a giant observation window. He clings to a gantry over the abyss—but Vader appears again, lightsaber aglow. In the ensuing fight, Vader lops off Luke's right hand, just as he himself had lost a forearm against Count Dooku years before.

That was when Vader was known as Anakin Skywalker— and that powerful secret is his final weapon against young Luke. "Obi-Wan never told you what happened to your father . . . . I am your father!"

More than a quarter of our fan survey respon- dents admitted they were "shocked" by Darth Vader's bombshell—"thoroughly gobsmacked" is how one described it. Another third said they were "pretty surprised," while only handful said they expected it—but some of them admitted they had already been tipped off: "Everyone ruined that scene for me because everybody always talks about it!"

Though there may have been hints to that point in the movies—"Search your feelings," Vader says, "you know it to be true"—it's an awful, horrifying revelation. Luke displays a punched-in-the-gut reaction like any of us who've faced a deeply personal disappointment: a friend has turned against you, a partner has been unfaithful, a church leader you trusted was exposed as a hypocrite, you name the pain.

It happened in Bible times, too. King David, "a man after [God's] own heart" (1 Samuel 13:14), committed adultery with Bathsheba—compounding the failure by having her husband killed (see 1 Samuel 11). Judas blatantly sold out Jesus (see Matthew 26:14–16). And after Jesus' arrest, Peter—one of His closest friends—denied even knowing Him (see Mark 14:66–72).

Major disappointments happen in a world where sin makes and keeps people selfish. Minor irritations occur all the time, even with the best of people. Be prepared to be disappointed . . . even with yourself sometimes. But know that there's one Person who will never harm or fail you in any way—Jesus, called "Faithful and True" (Revelation

19:11), "loves us and has freed us from our sins by his blood" (Revelation 1:5). No matter what happens, even when we stumble, "he remains faithful" (2 Timothy 2:13).

There are never shocking, depressing, or even mildly unpleasant surprises with Him.

I am convinced that neither death nor life, neither angels nor demons, neither the present nor the future, nor any powers, neither height nor depth, nor anything else in all creation, will be able to separate us from the love of God that is in Christ Jesus our Lord.

Romans 8:38–39

# HUMANOID

"Yousa no tinken yousa no greater
den da Gungans? Mesa lika dis!
Maybe wesa bein friends."

**Boss Nass,** *The Phantom Menace*

DOZENS OF SPECIES populate the *Star Wars* galaxy, many of them humanoid—resembling humans in some way, usually having a head, body, two arms, and a pair of legs. After that, the variety is vast.

From Chewbacca ("this big, walking carpet," in Leia's words) to Admiral Ackbar (a kind of Minotaur with a frog head), many are reminiscent of the old "What do you get when you cross . . .?" jokes: What do you get when you cross a professor with a lion? I don't know, but when he lectures, you'd better listen.

That would be true of Chewbacca, who Han Solo famously warned might "pull people's arms out of their sockets." The big Wookiee, the favorite non-human character in our fan survey, was prominent in Episodes IV, V, and VI but also appeared in *Revenge of the Sith,* fighting on his home planet of Kashyyyk alongside Yoda. Portrayed by seven-foot, four-inch Englishman Peter Mayhew, Chewbacca's distinctive "voice" was manufactured from recordings of animals, primarily bears.

An opposite of Chewbacca, at least in terms of hair, Admiral Ackbar came from the aquatic Mon Calamari race, favorite non-human characters of a few survey respondents. He commanded the assault on the second Death Star in the battle of Endor. Pop-eyed, with webbed hands, the admiral also appeared in our fan survey of favorite quotes with "It's a trap!"

Twi'leks aren't known for their hair, either, but for the tapering tentacles that grow from the backs of their heads. Their varying skin tones—blues and greens are common—also distinguish them from humans. Natives of the planet Ryloth, Twi'leks serve throughout the galaxy: Bib Fortuna was a kind of butler to Jabba the Hutt; Oola danced for the crime boss but died in the rancor pit for refusing to approach Jabba. Another female Twi'lek, Aayla Secura, was a Jedi knight in Episodes II and III who fell victim to Chancellor Palpatine's Order 66.

Many other humanoids appear in the series. Neimoidians, who lead the Trade Federation in prequel films; Gungans, such as Boss Nass and Jar Jar Binks; Jawas, the short, hooded beings with glowing yellow eyes; and scaly, green Rodians such as a boyhood friend of young Anakin Skywalker and the hapless bounty hunter Greedo, who made "the mess" in the Mos Eisley cantina.

Many *Star Wars* characters are made in a human image, much like humans are made in "the image of God" (Genesis 9:6). But just as many movie creatures lack human refinement, so humans come short of God's perfection.

Much of that is simply the gulf between Creator and created. But the difference is also sin, as the apostle Paul said of those who "exchanged the truth about God for a lie, and worshiped and served created things rather than the Creator" (Romans 1:25). The "godlessness and wickedness" Paul describes (Romans 1:18) can result in "envy, murder, strife, deceit and malice" (Romans 1:29). Or, as James notes, in seemingly smaller but still destructive attitudes like unkindness and hypocrisy: "With the tongue we praise our Lord and Father, and with it we curse human beings, who have been made in God's likeness" (James 3:9).

In that condition, like a lot of *Star Wars* humanoids, we're not a pretty sight. But God offers a way up, so we can better reflect His image to the world. "If anyone is in Christ," Paul wrote, "the new creation has come: The old has gone, the new is here!" (2 Corinthians 5:17).

We'll still struggle with sin, as Paul admitted in Romans 7, but with the Holy Spirit in our lives, we can "grow in the grace and knowledge of our Lord and Savior Jesus Christ" (2 Peter 3:18). We'll become less humanoid and more like God.

By one sacrifice [Jesus] has made perfect forever those who are being made holy.

Hebrews 10:14

# LUKE VS. EMPEROR

"Run, Luke! Run!"

**Ben Kenobi,** *Star Wars: A New Hope*

LUKE SKYWALKER was feeling pretty good about himself.

You could sense his satisfaction, even smugness, as he switched off his lightsaber and told the Emperor, "I'll never turn to the dark side." Darth Vader was on his hands and knees, weary and defeated. Rebel star fighters were preparing an attack on the second Death Star, where the three men faced off. "Soon, I'll be dead," Luke had calmly informed the Emperor, "and you with me."

He had certainly come a long way from his Tatooine moisture farm.

Luke Skywalker had learned the ways of the Force from the galaxy's last two Jedi. He'd had to convince Yoda he was more than an impatient, angry, and reckless adventurer, too old to begin schooling. When he quit his training early, unable to shake a vision of Han and Leia in peril, Luke left a ghostly Obi-Wan Kenobi pleading, "Don't give in to hate . . . that leads to the dark side."

He was tested in precisely that area. The Emperor goaded Luke, anticipating an angry reaction. "You want this, don't you?" the evil ruler murmured, holding up Luke's lightsaber. "The hate is swelling in you now. Take your Jedi weapon. Use it. I am unarmed. Strike me down with it. Give in to your anger."

Luke resisted the Emperor's prodding, as he did Darth Vader's—until father struck the nerve that sent his son raging. Tempting Luke to the dark side, Vader told the boy it was the only way to save his friends. "Your feelings for them are strong, especially for . . . sister," Vader mused. "So, you have a twin sister. If you will not turn to the dark side, then perhaps she will."

"No!" Luke shouted, attacking Vader with fury. Nothing that Yoda or Obi-Wan ever said could stop Luke's frenzied onslaught. The powerful Sith lord quickly succumbed, losing his prosthetic hand to Luke's lightsaber. But the sight of Vader's mechanical stump sobered Luke, who realized he had a similar hand. He stopped and tossed aside his weapon.

Having overcome his natural anger and aggression, Luke spared Vader's life and reproved the Emperor. "You've failed, Your Highness," Luke said proudly. "I am a Jedi, like my father before me."

Then the Emperor let him have it.

It seems Luke had been overconfident. He had learned much, as he'd told Yoda twice before. But the Emperor was truly much stronger. "Your feeble skills are no match for the power of the dark side," he growled, shooting bolt after painful bolt of Force lightning into Luke's body. "You have paid the price for your lack of vision."

Saved from death only by the surprising intervention of Darth Vader, Luke would have been wise to follow his teachers' advice, avoiding this confrontation until he was truly ready. As Christians, we should consider our limitations too.

There will be times to fight today's evil emperor, "the ruler of the kingdom of the air, the spirit who is now at work in those who are disobedient" (Ephesians 2:2). As the New Testament writer James wrote, "Resist the devil, and he will flee from you" (James 4:7).

But, on several occasions, the Bible also suggests that *we* do the running. "Flee from sexual immorality" (1 Corinthians 6:18). "Flee from idolatry" (1 Corinthians 10:14). "Flee the evil desires of youth" (2 Timothy 2:22). "Man of God, flee from all this" (1 Timothy 6:11), referring to false teaching and the love of money.

Maybe fleeing doesn't sound cool. But if your enemy is much stronger, fighting could be the worst choice you make. Run to God for safety, and let Him fight the battle for you. "The name of the LORD is a fortified tower; the righteous run to it and are safe" (Proverbs 18:10).

One day [Joseph] went into the house to attend to his duties, and none of the household servants was inside. [Potiphar's wife] caught him by his cloak and said, "Come to bed with me!" But he left his cloak in her hand and ran out of the house.

Genesis 39:11–12

# BAND OF WEIRDOS

"Did you hear that?"

**C-3PO,** *Star Wars: A New Hope*

THOUGH TATOOINE WAS a tough place to scratch out a living, some got by on a song.

In both the Mos Eisley cantina and Jabba's palace, musicians played for others' enjoyment. Their tunes weren't immediately what our earthbound ears expected, but the songs—composed and conducted by famed Hollywood musician John Williams—were soon more than just part of a movie soundtrack. They got into the collective memory of millions of moviegoers. So did the images of the players.

At Mos Eisley, where Obi-Wan Kenobi said one "must be cautious," the musicians are humanoid, with eyeballs like eight balls. Swaying to an alien jazz beat, they play instruments like oboes, performing a pair of songs in the background as Han Solo, Obi-Wan, and Luke Skywalker nego-tiate a fee for passage on the *Millennium Falcon*. Those songs were released as a stand-alone CD in 1997, a recording that identifies the band as Figrin D'an and the Modal Nodes.

In Jabba's lair, where one must be extremely cautious, another band plays. While the Modal Nodes appear like brothers from a large family, the Max Rebo Band is diverse. There's a pinkish, Pillsbury Doughboy type on the clarinet. There's a long-legged singer whose lips protrude from an equally long, anteater-style snout—she's called Sy Snootles in expanded universe material. And there's the keyboard-banging bandleader, Max Rebo, "a blue, flop-eared jizz wailer" as described in the *Return of the Jedi* novelization. (The first time I saw the film, I thought George Lucas had hijacked some kid's stuffed elephant for that scene.)

Let's face it: *Star Wars* musicians are a tad strange—not unlike the bands of people who gather in church on Sunday. Of course, Christians of every culture, all around the world, meet to worship in their own places, languages, and ways. But in the West, where believers are more likely to spend time on things like *Star Wars,* there's a temptation to view other people's churches as strange . . . or worse, wrong.

That's not to say that every church is correct. The Bible warns of false teachers who "secretly introduce destructive heresies, even denying the sovereign Lord who bought them" (2 Peter 2:1). But people who sincerely honor Jesus as God's Son, the sacrifice for sin, and the Lord of all are part of the *universal* church, "which is his body, the fullness of him who fills everything in every way" (Ephesians 1:23).

Not so long ago, many Christians looked askance at other believers who attended movies. Today, anyone who avoids the theater is considered strange by many fellow

Christians. Whether highly hip or overly old-fashioned, though, we're all part of the "body of Christ"—and we all owe each other respect.

"Just as a body, though one, has many parts, but all its many parts form one body, so it is with Christ," the apostle Paul said. "For we were all baptized by one Spirit so as to form one body—whether Jews or Gentiles, slave or free—and we were all given the one Spirit to drink. Even so the body is not made up of one part but of many . . . and each one of you is a part of it" (1 Corinthians 12:12–14, 27).

Sure, sometimes we're just a band of weirdos. But with practice, we can all offer God a harmonious song of worship.

The eye cannot say to the hand, "I don't need you!" And the head cannot say to the feet, "I don't need you!" On the contrary, those parts of the body that seem to be weaker are indispensable, and the parts that we think are less honorable we treat with special honor . . . . But God has put the body together, giving greater honor to the parts that lacked it, so that there should be no division in the body, but that its parts should have equal concern for each other.

1 Corinthians 12:21–23, 25

# INSIDE THE TAUNTAUN

"This may smell bad, kid.
But it'll keep you warm till I get the shelter up."

**Han Solo,** *The Empire Strikes Back*

MANY SCENES IN *STAR WARS* elicit *oohs*. This one gets an *ewww*.

After destroying the Death Star, the rebels returned to their base on Yavin 4 to celebrate. But they soon traded the temperate, forested moon for an icy planet called Hoth, where they established Echo Base.

The Hoth environment was so severe the rebels' speeders failed, so scouts domesticated a local lizard and used it for patrol duties. Something like a small T-rex, running on powerful hind legs, a tauntaun was big enough to hold a human on its back. Or, as we learned, in its gut.

Luke Skywalker was patrolling when an Imperial probe droid flashed down from the sky. Seeing it blast into a snowbank, he assumed it was a meteorite. Turning his tauntaun toward the impact to investigate, Luke and his mount were suddenly struck down by Hoth's version of the abominable snowman, the wampa.

With both nighttime and temperatures falling, Han Solo worried that Luke had failed to report in. So he climbed aboard a tauntaun and made for a base exit. Warned that his animal would freeze quickly in the worsening conditions—with the implication that Han would die with it—he responded, "Then I'll see you in hell!"

As Han began his search, Luke was awakening from the wampa's blow. In the creature's cave, hanging like a side of beef in a meat locker, Luke used the Force to regain his lightsaber, then cut himself down and fended off the wampa's next attack. Luke ran from the cave into the frigid night, falling facedown in the snow.

That's where Han discovered Luke, who was failing quickly. "Don't do this, Luke," Han pleaded while checking for breathing. "Come on, give me a sign, here." And at that point, Han's tauntaun gurgled and fell over dead.

Han paused just a moment to think, then pulled Luke toward the animal. Using Luke's lightsaber, he made a cut in the tauntaun's belly. Moviegoers could be thankful they only experienced the scene with two senses—sight and sound—as the results were truly disgusting. Han suffered through a third sense as he stuffed Luke into the creature's abdomen. "I thought they smelled bad," he gasped, "on the outside."

It was a disagreeable place, to be sure, but in reality the

safest spot for Luke. It was similar to some of the places God puts His own people.

Consider the apostle Paul, converted by the miraculous intervention of Jesus Himself, called God's "chosen instrument" (Acts 9:15), and author of at least thirteen of the New Testament's twenty-nine books. He also faced some amazingly tough circumstances. "I have worked much harder, been in prison more frequently, been flogged more severely, and been exposed to death again and again," he wrote to believers in Corinth. "Five times I received from the Jews the forty lashes minus one. Three times I was beaten with rods, once I was pelted with stones, three times I was shipwrecked . . . . I have labored and toiled and have often gone without sleep; I have known hunger and thirst and have often gone without food; I have been cold and naked" (2 Corinthians 11:23–25, 27).

Talk about a tauntaun's belly! And yet, Paul was never safer than when he was doing God's work. As he wrote to Christians in Philippi, "I desire to [die] and be with Christ, which is better by far; but it is more necessary for you that I remain in the body. Convinced of this, I know that I will remain" (Philippians 1:23–25).

Of course, Paul did ultimately die, just as each of us will. But that's only when God decides our work here is done. And then every *ewww* of earth becomes the *ooh* of heaven.

I know that through your prayers and God's provision of the Spirit of Jesus Christ what has happened to me will turn out for my deliverance.

Philippians 1:19

# THE CHOSEN ONE

"I know there is good in you."

**Luke Skywalker,** *Return of the Jedi*

YOU CAN CALL the *Star Wars* movies many things: exciting, groundbreaking, addictive. *Christian,* in the sense of being based in New Testament truth, would not be an adjective you'd probably use.

But, as we've seen throughout this book, many aspects of the series parallel characters, events, and principles from Scripture. And in the story of Anakin Skywalker, much of the terminology has a downright Christian sound.

Anakin was, in the opinion of Qui-Gon Jinn, "the chosen one," a fulfillment of prophecy, discovered by "the will of the Force." According to Anakin's mother, the child was a miracle of conception. "There was no father," Shmi Skywalker told Qui-Gon. "I carried him, I gave birth, I raised him. I can't explain what happened."

Qui-Gon sensed "something about this boy," telling Anakin's mother that she should be proud. "He gives without any thought of reward," the Jedi master said. "Well," Shmi replied, "he knows nothing of greed. He has—"

"He has special powers," Qui-Gon finished the thought. "He can see things before they happen." It was a Jedi trait, he continued, explaining Anakin's amazing reflexes and superhuman ability to race pods.

Shmi dreaded the podraces, which her greedy master made Anakin join. "I don't want you to race," she told him. "I die every time Watto makes you do it." But when it became clear that Anakin's talent would allow Qui-Gon and Obi-Wan to leave Tatooine and save Naboo, she relented. "I may not like it, but he can help you," she said. "He was meant to help you."

The more Qui-Gon and Shmi talked, the clearer Anakin's life mission became. The boy himself sensed hints of that mission. "I had a dream I was a Jedi," he told Qui-Gon. "I came back here and freed all the slaves." After his almost miraculous podrace victory, Shmi told him, "You have brought hope to those who have none."

At some point in our lives, all of us are "without hope" (Ephesians 2:12). In our world—the real world—it's Jesus who brings hope to those who have none. To everyone who believes in Him, "God has chosen to make known . . . the glorious riches of this mystery, which is Christ in you, the hope of glory" (Colossians 1:27).

Jesus is "the chosen one." He is God's anointed— *Messiah* in Hebrew, *Christ* in Greek—sent to save us from sin. His birth fulfilled several prophecies, including one of a miraculous origin: "The virgin will conceive and give birth to a son" (Isaiah 7:14). He came "to set the oppressed free" (Luke 4:18), breaking our slavery to sin. He demonstrated many "special powers," healing the sick, raising the dead, reading people's minds. He gave without thought of reward, offering "his life as a ransom for many" (Mark 10:45). He was meant to help others, and "did not come to be served, but to serve" (Matthew 20:28).

Ultimately, Jesus' life mission brings up another *Star Wars* parallel, the theme of redemption. But here there's a dramatic difference. Anakin Skywalker chose the dark side and, as Darth Vader, *needed* redemption. Jesus lived a perfect life, then died as a sacrifice to *offer* redemption.

In the end, Darth Vader redeemed himself, "coming out of his evil hibernation and being reborn as Anakin Skywalker," in George Lucas's words. Jesus redeemed others, people who had absolutely no ability to buy their own way out of sin. "When we were still powerless," the apostle Paul wrote, "Christ died for the ungodly" (Romans 5:6).

Through Jesus, all the galaxies were created (John 1:3), humans are reconciled to God (Romans 5:10), and eternal life can be enjoyed (John 3:16). He does so much more than bring balance to some universal force. Jesus is the *real* Force.

God exalted him to the highest place and gave him the name that is above every name, that at the name of Jesus every knee should bow, in heaven and on earth and under the earth, and every tongue acknowledge that Jesus Christ is Lord, to the glory of God the Father.

Philippians 2:9–11

## ACKNOWLEDGMENTS

IN CREATING THIS BOOK, I appreciated the input of dozens of *Star Wars* aficionados who participated in the fan survey. I especially enjoyed the friendship, encouragement, and insights of Andy Rogers, Ed Strauss, Greg Johnson, Kelly McIntosh, and Todd Smith. The Worthy Publishing team of Pamela Clements, Hampton Ryan, Marilyn Janson and Bart Dawson have also been tremendously helpful. You have all improved this project in many ways, and I appreciate each of you. Of course, any errors in the book (hopefully, very few) are solely mine.

## ABOUT THE AUTHOR

PAUL KENT is the author of eight books and contributor to or coauthor of numerous others. His goal is to make the Bible more interesting and accessible to readers of all ages and backgrounds. Paul has loved the Star Wars saga since he saw the original movie poster at age 11 . . . though his parents didn't let him see the film until a year later! Paul and his wife, Laurie, also a Star Wars fan, have adopted three children and live near Grand Rapids, Michigan.

## IF YOU ENJOYED THIS BOOK, WILL YOU CONSIDER SHARING THE MESSAGE WITH OTHERS?

Mention the book in a blog post or through Facebook, Twitter, Pinterest, or upload a picture through Instagram.

Recommend this book to those in your small group, book club, workplace, and classes.

Head over to facebook.com/worthypublishing, "LIKE" the page, and post a comment as to what you enjoyed the most.

Tweet "I recommend reading #TheRealForce by Paul Kent // @worthypub"

Pick up a copy for someone you know who would be challenged and encouraged by this message.

Write a book review online.

**WORTHY®**
PUBLISHING

**Visit us at worthypublishing.com**

twitter.com/worthypub

worthypub.tumblr.com

facebook.com/worthypublishing

pinterest.com/worthypub

instagram.com/worthypub

youtube.com/worthypublishing